ROADMAP™ B1+

WORKBOOK
with key and online audio

Rebecca Adlard, Anna Osborn

CONTENTS

3

Vocabulary

Eating out

1 Match the words in the box with definitions 1–8.

> allergic   delicious   packed   service   set menu
> spicy   terrace   ~~vegetarian~~

1 someone who never eats meat or fish   *vegetarian*
2 when someone brings your food or drinks in a café or restaurant   _____
3 when something makes you ill if you eat it or touch it
   _____
4 an area next to a building where people can sit outside to eat
5 strongly flavoured with spices   _____
6 food that tastes very nice   _____
7 extremely crowded   _____
8 a short list of meals in a restaurant or café at a fixed price   _____

2 Choose the correct alternatives.

> I went to the new Spanish place with my friend last night. It was so **1**_packed/_ delicious that we had to share a table with some other people. The **2**service/ set menu was good value, but every main course included meat or fish. I'm **3**vegetarian/ decent, so that was no good for me. Instead, I chose baked cheese with honey, which was **4**delicious/ quality. My friend had a meat dish, which had lots of spices in it. I thought it was too **5**spicy/ allergic, but he enjoyed it. After our meal, we had coffee on the **6**service/ terrace, which was very nice. The outdoor **7**heaters/ menu were on, so we were lovely and warm. The meal came to just under 25 euros for each of us, which we both thought was good **8**order/ value.

3 Rewrite the sentences using the words in brackets so that they mean the same.

1 I can't eat cheese because it makes me ill.
   I'm ____*allergic to cheese*____ . (allergic)
2 My sister doesn't eat meat.
   My sister _____ . (vegetarian)
3 Shall I make a reservation for dinner on Saturday night?
   Shall I _____ ? (book in advance)
4 The waiter yesterday evening was fantastic.
   We _____ . (service)
5 We were there for an hour before we got a table.
   We waited _____ . (ages)
6 Three courses with a drink costs £15.
   The _____ . (set menu)
7 It cost a lot more than the previous time we were there.
   They have definitely _____ . (prices)
8 The menu is excellent. I think you could take anyone there.
   I think the place _____ . (suit)

4 Complete the sentences with the missing words.

1 I was annoyed when the waiter got our o_rder_ _____ wrong and brought me fish instead of steak.
2 If you like spicy food, try the new Indian p_____ on the high street.
3 I don't suppose you f_____ pizza tonight, do you?
4 I thought the restaurant was excellent. We had great service and t_____ quality food!
5 The set menu was fifteen euros for three courses and the plates were huge. It was very good v_____ .
6 I really appreciate it when restaurants offer p_____ of choice for vegetarians.

Grammar

Noun phrases 1

5 Match the sentence halves.

1 I'm going to get a coffee   *d*
2 The pasta that my friend ordered   _____
3 The café across the road   _____
4 Can I book a table   _____
5 That's the café   _____
6 The Italian waiter   _____

a was too spicy.
b by the window?
c who served us spoke very good English.
d to take away.
e sells amazing cakes.
f where I first met my boyfriend.

6 Complete the sentences with one word.

1 This is the first dish _____ my mother taught me how to cook.
2 This is my Grandma, _____ is allergic to spicy food.
3 Let's try that new restaurant _____ the old town.
4 I'm looking for a nice vegetarian restaurant _____ take my sister to for dinner.
5 *Cheneys* is the best place _____ have breakfast.
6 Shall we meet at the café _____ to the cathedral?
7 That's the restaurant _____ Jon used to work.
8 Espresso is the best kind of coffee _____ have after lunch.

Vocabulary

Where I live

1 Choose the correct option a, b or c.

Last month I moved **1**_____ of my parents' house in a quiet village and moved **2**_____ with one of my friends in the city. I was sad to move **3**_____ from the place where I grew up, but I love living in the city. Our apartment is surrounded **4**_____ lively cafés and restaurants. It's in quite an old building and the landlord was talking about knocking it **5**_____ last year. Luckily, they decided not to do that in the end. The landlord decorated the apartment and put **6**_____ central heating, so now it's very comfortable. We could do **7**_____ a bit more space in the bedrooms, but the location is great and it feels like home. I just hope that the landlord doesn't put **8**_____ the rent now because it already costs us a fortune.

1	**a** away	**b** out	**c** off
2	**a** in	**b** on	**c** into
3	**a** away	**b** to	**c** in
4	**a** to	**b** around	**c** by
5	**a** up	**b** in	**c** down
6	**a** in	**b** away	**c** on
7	**a** on	**b** up	**c** with
8	**a** in	**b** up	**c** on

2 Complete the sentences with the words in the box.

cost	do	freezing	knock down	~~landlord~~	storage
tidy	tiny				

1 My _landlord_ is really kind. He doesn't mind if we're late with our rent.
2 The flat is never messy because we always keep it clean and _____ .
3 You could _____ this wall and make the kitchen bigger.
4 There's isn't much _____ in Paula's kitchen, so she's going to get some new cupboards.
5 This bedroom is so _____ that there's not even enough room for a bed!
6 It's _____ in here. Can I put the central heating on?
7 Let me pay for half the rent because it's only fair that we share the _____ .
8 I could _____ with a spare bed so that my friends can stay.

Grammar

Modifying comparisons

3 Put the words in the correct order to make sentences.

1 a lot / than / my village / more exciting / This city / is
   This city is a lot more exciting than my village.
2 slightly / This place / better / is / my last apartment / in / condition / than
   _____
3 much / than / other neighbourhoods / Chelsea / is / livelier
   _____
4 to live / a bit / than / I'd like / here / cheaper / somewhere
   _____
5 even / is / than / The bedroom / tinier / the living room
   _____
6 isn't / This apartment / nearly / my brother's / expensive / as / as
   _____

4 Choose the correct alternatives.

1 Marc is 160 cm tall and Tom is 162 cm tall. Tom is *much/slightly* taller than Marc.
2 Lauren is 74 years old and Sarah is 18. Lauren is a *lot/bit* older than Sarah.
3 Kim's bedroom is huge and Sam's bedroom is tiny. Kim's bedroom is *much/slightly* larger than Sam's.
4 Tina pays $100 rent a week and Zak pays $105 rent a week. Tina's rent isn't *quite/nearly* as expensive as Zak's.
5 Hassan's room is very tidy and Valerie's is tidier than Hassan's. Valerie's room is *quite/even* tidier than Hassan's.
6 My old neighbourhood was boring, but this area isn't boring at all. This neighbourhood is *nearly/far* more interesting than my old one.

5 Find and correct five mistakes in sentences 1–8.

1 My parents' house is much ~~big~~ *bigger* than mine.
2 This area isn't nearly as expensive as some parts of the capital.
3 My neighbourhood is bit quieter than some areas.
4 This apartment isn't nearly larger enough for all of us.
5 The village was a lot livelier than the town.
6 Kerry's apartment is much tidy than Martin's.
7 The bedroom at the back of the house isn't quite as bigger as the bedroom at the front.
8 This neighbourhood is even rougher than where Jack used to live!

Vocabulary
Going out, staying in

1 **Choose the correct alternatives.**

A: Shall we stay **1** *in/on* and watch TV or go **2** *in/out* for dinner tonight?

B: It depends. I might not get home **3** *till/by* after seven. I don't want to stay **4** *in/up* really late because I've got a meeting first thing in the morning.

A: Well, if you get home early enough, we could go out for an early dinner. We can go to a restaurant where we don't have to queue to get **5** *on/in* and we don't have to go **6** *on/up* to anywhere else afterwards. We can come straight home and then you won't get **7** *up/to* bed too late.

B: OK, sounds good. Oh no! I'm late for work. Please could you tidy **8** *on/up* these plates for me?

A: Of course I can! See you later.

2 **Complete the sentences with the words in the box.**

celebrate	episode	fortune	home
missed	play	queue	~~talking~~
throwing	worth		

1 I got ____*talking*____ to my friend Peter and forgot what time it was.

2 We didn't have to _____ to get in to the restaurant because they found us a table right away.

3 We're _____ a surprise party next week for my parents' anniversary.

4 How are you going to _____ your birthday?

5 I want to stay in tonight and watch the next _____ of my favourite series.

6 I'm so tired this morning, but it's _____ it because I had a great time yesterday evening!

7 We _____ the last bus yesterday evening, so we had to get a taxi home.

8 I hope Sue likes her present because it cost me a _____ .

9 What time do you think you'll get _____ from the party?

10 Tomorrow I'm going to watch my friend who is in a _____ at our local theatre.

Grammar
Non-defining relative clauses

3 **Choose the correct option a, b or c.**

Last night I went to a party, **1** _____ I met some really interesting people. There were a lot of students there, **2** _____ are here on exchange programmes from different countries. There was a girl called Mei from Beijing, **3** _____ is here for three months. She wants to work in China as an English teacher, which is **4** _____ she's come here to improve her English. I also met a man called Richard, **5** _____ son is an actor. He's going to be in a play **6** _____ starts next month, called *The End of Time*. It sounds really interesting. Richard is going to get me a ticket on Tuesday, **7** _____ they go on sale. The play is at the National Theatre, **8** _____ we watched that Shakespeare play last year.

1	**a** who	**b** where	**c** which
2	**a** when	**b** most of whom	**c** why
3	**a** who	**b** whose	**c** which is why
4	**a** when	**b** why	**c** where
5	**a** who	**b** whose	**c** most of whom
6	**a** which	**b** when	**c** where
7	**a** which	**b** where	**c** when
8	**a** which is why	**b** where	**c** which

4 **Combine the sentences with a relative pronoun.**

1 Last night I went to watch a ballet. It was brilliant.
   Last night I went to watch a ballet, which was brilliant.

2 I threw a party for Rachel. Her birthday is next week.
   _____

3 Samira went to the opera in Paris. She saw *Tosca*.
   _____

4 I queued behind a lot of people. Most of the people already had tickets.
   _____

5 I stayed up late last night. That's why I was tired this morning.
   _____

6 John studied in Madrid. He met his girlfriend there.
   _____

7 We're going to miss the last metro. This means we'll have to get a taxi.
   _____

8 Dan and I went to a cafe before the show. The show didn't start until three o'clock .
   _____

Functional language

Express preferences and give reasons

1 Complete conversations 1–4 with sentences a–h.

1 A: Lisa, have a look at these two hotels I've found online. **1** _e_ .

B: Both of them look nice. You can choose, **2** _____ .

2 A: Hey, Marvin, where would you rather be – in the city or in the countryside?

B: **3** _____ . Cities are stressful and there's not much to do in the countryside.

A: So where would you prefer to be?

B: **4** _____ .

3 A: Fran, we'd love you to come on holiday with us this summer to *Beach Bay* caravan park.

B: Thanks, Mum, but to be honest, *Beach Bay* looks very quiet. **5** _____

A: Really? I think you'd love it. It's right by the sea. **6** _____ .

4 A: Dan, if you don't want to go to a Greek island where do you want to go on holiday?

B: **7** _____ .

A: Why would you like to go to a city?

B: **8** _____ .

a Neither of them are my kind of place, to be honest.

b I don't think it's my kind of place.

c We'd have lots to see and do, whereas on an island we'd be stuck in one place.

d I'd rather be by the beach.

e Which one do you prefer?

f I don't have any strong feelings either way.

g You could probably go diving there.

h If it was just up to me, I'd go to London.

2 Match the sentence halves.

1 You'd be able to _____ _b_

2 It looks like the kind of town _____

3 I'd prefer not _____

4 If it was just up to me, _____

5 Backpacking is my kind of _____

6 If you had to choose, _____

7 I'd rather _____

8 I like _____

a to go on holiday in August.

b practise your English.

c the idea of travelling by train rather than by plane.

d holiday.

e which car would you buy?

f we'd be happy to live in.

g I'd stay in a tent not a hotel.

h go to a place which has few tourists.

Listening

1 🔊 1.01 **Listen to the first part of a radio programme. Where is Onni from?**

a Norway　　**b** France　　**c** Finland

2 **Listen to the first part again and choose the correct alternatives.**

1 The radio programme is called *Nights on Earth / Day and Night*.

2 There are *two / three* different kinds of night where Onni lives.

3 The nights in winter are called the *dark / polar* nights.

3 🔊 1.02 **Listen to the second part of the radio programme. Are the sentences true (T) or false (F)?**

1 People don't sleep much in the winter. _____

2 Most people just sleep through the polar nights. _____

3 Nobody gets sad in the winter. _____

4 Artificial lights can help to reduce the negative effects of the lack of daylight. _____

5 Onni recommends keeping busy in the winter. _____

6 Onni believes that visitors are less affected by polar nights than the people who live there. _____

7 In the summer, the sun doesn't set for two months. _____

8 Nobody goes fishing in the middle of the night during the white nights. _____

4a **Complete the summary with words from the radio programme.**

In the winter, the sun doesn't **1** _____ for **2** _____ months. It gets dark in **3** _____ and doesn't get light again until **4** _____ .

In the **5** _____ , the opposite happens. The sun doesn't **6** _____ for **7** _____ months. So there is no **8** _____ time.

b **Listen again and check.**

1

Reading

1 Read the article and choose the best title.

a Tips for moving house

b Original homes from around the world

c A skateboarder's dream home

2 Read the article again. Match comments 1–3 with houses in the article, a–c.

1 │ The most important thing for me is light and space.

2 │ I like finding houses in unusual places in cities. A house doesn't have to be big to be beautiful.

3 │ I love sport, so I'd like a house where I can always do something active, both inside and outside!

a Keret House _____

b The Skateboard House _____

c House NA _____

3 Read the article again and complete the text.

The Skateboard House is in
¹ _California, USA_ . It was the idea of
Pierre André Snizergues and it has got
² _____ different living areas.
You can skate everywhere in the house –
over the ³ _____ .
House NA is in ⁴ _____ ,
It has got ⁵ _____ floors. These
are all at a different ⁶ _____
from each other, like the branches of a tree.
This idea comes from the
⁷ _____ Japanese belief that
trees are very important.
Keret House is in ⁸ _____ .
The designer was Jakub Szczęsny, an
architect and ⁹ _____ . It is
¹⁰ _____ wide at its narrowest
point and it has got ¹¹ _____
floors.

Moving house can be very exciting, but it can also be difficult if you can't find the kind of home you are looking for. Some people have clear ideas about their dream homes, so they hire architects to design and build unusual, interesting and **original** houses, especially for them.

Every keen skateboarder dreams about turning his or her home into a skatepark, surrounded by **smooth** areas which are perfect for skateboarding. Pierre André Snizergues, a former world skateboarding champion, made his dream come true by building The Skateboard House in California, USA. The design of the house means that you can skate everywhere, inside and outside. The house has got one floor with three separate areas – a living area, a sleeping area and a skateboard practice area. In each part of the house you can skate all the way up the walls to the ceiling. You can even skate over the furniture. In addition, the house is **eco-friendly**, with all energy coming from the sun and the wind.

Another unusual home is House NA in Tokyo, Japan. It's different from other houses because it has got huge windows instead of walls. Because you can see through the house's walls, it's very **bright**, with plenty of natural light. The architects, Sou Fujimoto Architects, got the idea for their design from an **ancient** Japanese belief that trees are very important. The house has got three floors, with stairs and ladders connecting them. The floors are like the branches of a tree, each at a different height, so you can be in one part of the house, but you can hear and see what's going on in another part of the house.

One challenge of modern city living is finding new spaces to live within crowded neighbourhoods. Architect and artist Jakub Szczęsny designed Keret House in Warsaw, Poland. He chose to build the house in a tiny space between two buildings from different periods of history. It's certainly **cosy** – the narrowest point of Keret House is 92 cm and the widest point is 152 cm, making it the thinnest house in the world. The house has got two floors, with a ladder leading from one to the other, and there's a bedroom, a kitchen, a bathroom and a living area. **Stylish** glass walls also mean that there is plenty of light in the house.

These houses may be more interesting than **traditional** homes, but would they be good places to live in?

Would you choose to live in any of these three houses? Why not share your ideas in the comments box.

4 Read the article again and answer the questions.

1 Why do some people design and build their own houses?
Because they have clear ideas about their dream houses.

2 Who is Pierre André Snizergues?

3 Where can you skate in the house he designed?

4 How does Snizergues's house help to protect the environment?

5 Why is House NA unusual?

6 Where did the architects of House NA get the idea for their design?

7 Why was Jakub Szczęsny's house a challenge to build?

8 How did he make his house as bright as possible?

5 Match the words in bold in the article with definitions 1–8.

1 something that has existed for a long time without changing
traditional

2 comfortable and warm

3 good for the environment

4 full of light, not dark

5 attractive and fashionable

6 something that isn't copied from something else

7 very, very old

8 not rough

6 Read the comment box. Which of the three houses in the article does Josh like best?

7 Read the comment box again and choose the correct option, a, b or c.

1 Josh has just read an article about unusual ____ .
a homes
b people
c holidays

2 Josh would like to stay in ____ .
a The Skateboard House
b The NA House
c The Keret House

3 He thinks that the House NA ____ .
a is a crazy idea
b must be full of light
c could be a wonderful place to live

4 He thinks that Keret House ____ .
a is designed in a clever way
b is a place he'd like to live
c seems a great space

5 He lives in ____ .
a an unusual house
b an interesting house
c a normal house

6 When he goes on holiday, he likes to stay in ____ .
a hotels
b normal houses
c unusual houses

7 When he stayed in a treehouse, he ____ .
a enjoyed being close to nature
b fell out of the tree
c couldn't sleep at night

WHAT DO YOU THINK?

1 comment   Josh · December 9 · 9.15 a.m.

I really enjoyed reading about these unusual houses. House NA is an interesting idea and the house must be lovely and bright. However, I don't really like the idea of everyone being able to see what I'm doing. Keret House is a clever design, but space is very important for me, so I don't think I could stay inside that house for very long. I like skateboarding, so I'd like to stay in The Skateboard House. It sounds amazing!

My home isn't very interesting. It's just a normal house! But my girlfriend and I like to stay in unusual houses when we go on holiday.

Last summer, we stayed in a treehouse for three nights. The rooms were built around the trunk of a tree! It was amazing to be part of the natural world, but you have to be careful you don't fall out during the night! Luckily that didn't happen to us!

Josh, Toronto

Writing

1 **Read the email types and write *formal* or *informal*.**
An email to:

1 your aunt to ask her advice about birthday presents.
....

2 your boss to ask if you can have next Tuesday off work.
....

3 a client to ask them to send you some information.
....

4 a restaurant to ask for a reservation. ....

5 a friend to invite them to a party. ....

6 your brother to ask him to pick your father up tomorrow.
....

7 a language school to ask them to send you registration details. ....

8 a hotel to ask if they have any rooms free next weekend.
....

2 **Read the emails and answer the questions.**

1 Email 1: is the email formal or informal? Why did Tina write it?
....
....

2 Email 2: is the email formal or informal? Why did Tina write it?
....
....
....

---

1 Dear Sir/Madam,

Further to my conversation this morning with Mrs James, I am writing to confirm my reservation for six double bedrooms for the 17th and 18th August.

I have a few additional requests. Firstly, I was wondering if we could have rooms with a view of the garden.

Secondly, our group includes my grandmother, who is 88. I would be most grateful if you could give us one room on the ground floor, so that my grandmother doesn't have to walk up any stairs.

Finally, as this is my parents' anniversary party, we would like to give them a special celebration cake with their names (Mary and John) on it. Do you think you could possibly prepare this for us? If so, would you mind letting me know how much this will cost? Would it be possible to let me know about the cake by the end of the week?

I look forward to hearing from you soon.

Best regards,

Tina Manson

---

2 Hi everyone,

Hope you are all well.

Not long now till my mum and dad's 25th anniversary weekend! Hope you're all looking forward to it! We're so glad that you can join us.

Just a quick email to say I've booked the rooms in the hotel for 17th and 18th August. The reservation is for six double bedrooms, so if any of you can no longer make it, then please email me back asap. Also, if you think you might only be able to stay one night, can you let me know so I can tell the hotel?

One more thing, I'm making a special album of photos from over the years. Does anyone have any photos we could use? If you have, could you send them over to me this week so I can get them printed in the album?

Remember that it's a surprise weekend for my parents, so don't say anything to them about any of this! I'll email you again nearer the time and let you know exactly what time we'll be arriving with Mum and Dad. Then you can all jump out and surprise them when we get there! Can't wait to see their faces!

Cheers,

Tina

3 Read the emails again. Are the statements below true (T) or false (F)?

1 Tina's parents are celebrating their 16th wedding anniversary on 17th and 18th August. _F_

2 Tina is organising the weekend for her parents. _____

3 She reserved six bedrooms. _____

4 She asks the hotel to give them rooms with a view of the sea. _____

5 She asks the hotel to make special arrangements for her grandfather. _____

6 Tina's parents are called Mary and John. _____

7 She asks the hotel restaurant to make a special cake. _____

8 She asks friends to send her photographs for a special video that she's making. _____

4 Match Tina's requests with Email 1 or 2.

1 She wants to receive photos of Mary and John.
_____

2 She wants rooms that look over the garden.
_____

3 She wants a cake with Mary and John's names on it. _____

4 She wants guests to confirm that they are still coming.
_____

5 She wants to know if any guests can only stay one night.
_____

6 She wants a ground floor room for her grandmother.
_____

5 Read the Focus box. Then underline phrases in the emails which are used to make formal and informal requests.

Making requests in emails

When you ask for things – or ask people to do things for you – in more formal emails, you tend to use longer phrases.

Would it be possible to stay an extra night?
I would be (most) grateful if you could email me the details.
Do you think you could (possibly) send me written confirmation of my booking?
I was wondering if we could have our own private room.
Would you mind moving us to a bigger table?

In more informal emails, you can just use *could* or *can*.
Could/Can you (please) let me know if you can make it?

You can also use imperatives. Make imperatives sound softer by adding please.
(Please) call me as soon as you hear anything.

After requests, you often explain why you were asking.
If you've got any special requests, could you send them over to me this week so I can get a final list to the restaurant ahead of time.

6 Complete the missing words to make requests.

1 I would be most g _rateful_ if you could send me the vegetarian menu.

2 Would it be p_____ to have a table outside?

3 I was w_____ if you have a vegan menu?

4 Would you m_____ preparing a special dish without nuts?

5 Do you t_____ you could let us stay until midnight?

6 C_____ you please make sure we have a table away from the door?

7 Could y_____ prepare a special set menu for us?

8 P_____ send me confirmation asap.

7 Answer the questions about the two emails.

1 Which greeting starts the email?
Formal   _Dear Sir/Madam_
Informal _____

2 Which phrase explains why the person is writing?
Formal _____
_____

Informal _____
_____

3 Are contractions used (e.g. *I'm, you're,* etc.)? If so, give examples.
Formal _____
Informal _____

4 Which phrase ends the email?
Formal _____
Informal _____

Prepare

8 You're organising a special holiday with a group of friends. Plan two emails that make requests – one email to the hotel where you're staying, and the other email to invite your friends. Make notes that answer these questions:

- What is the purpose of the holiday?
- Where are you going?
- What two requests would you like to make to the hotel?
- What two requests would you like to make to your friends?

Write

9 Write the two emails. Use your notes in Exercise 8 and the Focus box to help you.

2A

Vocabulary
Learning new skills

1 Choose the correct alternatives.

I always enjoy trying **1**on/*out* new instruments because I'm really keen **2**at/*on* music. I play the piano and the flute, and at the moment I'm having a go **3**out/*at* learning the violin. It's a bit **4**of/*off* a challenge and I'm useless **5**on/*at* it, but it doesn't matter! I go **6**over/*out* what I learn during the lessons and I practise every day. I think that I've got a long way **7**for/*to* go, but my teacher says I'm making a lot **8**of/*on* progress.

2 Match the sentence halves.

1 I'm downloading ___d___
2 We're doing _____
3 He's developing _____
4 They're making _____
5 I have _____
6 She's trying _____
7 He's keen _____
8 I'm useless _____

a his technique in football.
b a lot of progress in learning to play the cello.
c out her cycling skills.
d an app, which will help me to learn Chinese.
e on learning French.
f a long way to go before I can ride a motorbike.
g at learning new languages.
h a language exchange with some Italian students.

3 Complete the sentences with the words in the box.

| challenge | ~~develop~~ | expert | improve | interested |
| keen | skilled | training | | |

1 I practise skateboarding every day so that I can _develop_ my technique.
2 I'm _____ a lot because I want to run a ten-kilometre race next month.
3 John has been working hard to _____ his computer skills.
4 Nala is highly _____ at painting. She had her own art exhibition last month.
5 My mum has taught my sister to cook over the years and now she's a bit of an _____ .
6 Diving is something that has always _____ me.
7 I'm making some progress with Mandarin, but it's a bit of a _____ .
8 Jane's _____ on music, so I think she'll enjoy learning to play the piano.

Grammar
Present simple and present continuous

4 Find and correct five mistakes in sentences 1–8.

train
1 I ~~am training~~ at the sports centre every Tuesday and Thursday.
2 Some young people are starting to write letters instead of sending emails.
3 Ashanti downloads an app at the moment.
4 Are you understanding what I mean?
5 The word 'expert' is meaning someone who is good at something.
6 She's having a go at the guitar this term.
7 Yin and Michael are belonging to a golf club.
8 I don't believe that's true.

5 Complete the conversation. Use the present simple or present continuous form of the verbs in brackets.

A: Hi Dan, what **1** _are_ you _doing_ (do) in the kitchen? You **2** _____ (hate) cooking!
B: I **3** _____ (have) a go at making an omelette!
A: Really?
B: Yes, I **4** _____ (do) a cookery course this month and I **5** _____ (go) over what we learnt in the last class.
A: Good for you! I've heard that lots of people **6** _____ (do) cookery courses at the moment.
B: Yes, my course is very popular. Anyway, I **7** _____ (feel) that I'm useless at cooking, so it's a bit of a challenge.
A: I **8** _____ (not think) you're useless. The food smells really good! Fish **9** _____ (not be) easy to cook.
B: OK, it's ready now. **10** _____ you _____ (want) to join me?
A: Yes, please!

Vocabulary
Starting work

1 Complete the text with the words in the box.

| casual | fire | first | ~~flexible~~ | formal | health |
| strict | time |

I really like my boss. She's **1** _flexible_ about the hours we work. We can change the **2** _____ of our lunch break as long as we talk to her first. We can also change our holiday dates right up to the last minute. However, she does have a **3** _____ policy about clothes. We have to wear **4** _____ clothes at the office. We aren't allowed to wear **5** _____ dress, such as jeans. My boss is also careful about **6** _____ and safety rules. She makes sure that we have regular **7** _____ drills and everyone has to do a **8** _____ aid course.

2 Choose the correct option a, b or c.

1 I'm not happy about the way my boss treats me. I'm going to contact my __b__ representative.
   a rules **b** union **c** course

2 There isn't a real fire. It's just a fire _____ .
   a policy **b** course **c** drill

3 All the union _____ came to the meeting about the strike.
   a people **b** members **c** drills

4 The health and _____ rules protect people when they are at work.
   a safe **b** safer **c** safety

5 I work the night _____ every Saturday.
   a shift **b** time **c** drill

6 Sarah did a _____ course so that she knows what to do if someone is sick at the office.
   a safety **b** policy **c** first aid

7 After you've met all the employees, I'll show you around the _____ .
   a shift **b** site **c** rules

8 The company has quite _____ working hours. We don't have to start work at 9 a.m. every day.
   a flexible **b** smart **c** practice

Grammar
Present habits

3 Put the words in the correct order to make sentences.

1 tend / the office / people / to / by 9 a.m. / get / to / Most
   Most people tend to get to the office by 9 a.m.

2 first aid courses / We / staff / offer / regularly / to
   _____

3 a habit / of / has / computer / This / crashing
   _____

4 union meetings / time / have / We / time / to / from
   _____

5 there's / on / As / a strict policy / recycling / a rule
   _____

6 doesn't / Philippe / time off / January / tend / to take / in
   _____

7 casual / on / normally / clothes / Employees / Fridays / wear
   _____

8 don't / 6 p.m. / We / to work / after / tend
   _____

4 Read the sentences and tick the correct meaning a or b.

1 Lucy eats in the canteen from time to time.
   a Lucy eats in the canteen once or twice a month. ✓
   b Lucy eats in the canteen every day.

2 People are regularly changing shifts.
   a People often change shifts.
   b People don't often change shifts.

3 As a rule, the manager holds a staff meeting every Monday.
   a The manager sometimes holds a staff meeting on Mondays.
   b The manager usually holds a staff meeting on Mondays.

4 This printer has a habit of breaking down.
   a This printer often breaks down.
   b This printer rarely breaks down.

5 Staff tend to take holidays in August.
   a Staff usually take holidays in August.
   b Staff never take holidays in August.

6 Aisha is constantly late for work.
   a Aisha is sometimes late for work.
   b Aisha is late for work every day.

7 Employees don't tend to take a lunch break.
   a Employees usually take a lunch break.
   b Employees don't usually take a lunch break.

8 On the whole, employees eat in the staff canteen.
   a Employees mostly eat in the staff canteen.
   b Employees occasionally eat in the staff canteen.

2c

Grammar

used to, *would* and past simple

1 **Choose the correct option a , b or c.**

When I was a young boy, life **1**_____ less complicated than it is now. My brother and I **2**_____ with our toys outside in the street and my parents **3**_____ worry about us. During the summer holidays, my mother **4**_____ us a picnic and we **5**_____ our bikes into the forest for the whole day. Once, I **6**_____ off my bike and my brother **7**_____ all the way home to tell my parents. Those experiences **8**_____ us to become independent.

1	a	is	b	has been	c used to be
2	a	use to play	b	used to play	c used play
3	a	don't	b	didn't use to	c didn't used to
4	a	make	b	would make	c made
5	a	have ridden	b	ride	c would ride
6	a	fell	b	used to fall	c would fall
7	a	rode	b	used to ride	c would ride
8	a	taught	b	was teaching	c used to teach

2 **Find and correct five mistakes in sentences 1–8.**

> *broke*

1 I ~~used to break~~ my arm when we were on holiday in Greece in 2014.

2 When I was young, I used to deliver newspapers in my neighbourhood.

3 I would live in Spain when I was a child.

4 Julia didn't never use to play the piano.

5 My friends and I would play on the beach all day when we were young.

6 One time, I would see a jellyfish in the sea!

7 Toby didn't use to play tennis when he was young.

8 Did you used to walk to school when you were a child?

Vocabulary

Parents and children

3 **Complete in the sentences with the missing words.**

1 We should c *ontrol*_____ how much children use technology. They're too young to know when to switch it off.

2 My mum used to f_____ me to eat everything on my plate. Now I'm grown up, I eat anything!

3 I don't think we should w_____ over children all the time. They need to learn how to look after themselves.

4 Some parents make too many a_____ for their children. They don't have any free time.

5 I always l_____ my children play outside because we live in a very safe neighbourhood.

6 We must respect people in a_____ because otherwise there would be no law and order.

7 I teach my children the importance of good m_____ . They always say 'please' and 'thank you'.

8 When he was a child, my brother always used to get into t_____ , but now he's older, he behaves really well!

4 **Match the sentence halves.**

1 I always used to get   _h_

2 It's important for children to learn good   _____

3 Can you entertain   _____

4 We mustn't watch   _____

5 We all experience   _____

6 Life is more   _____

7 She doesn't let   _____

8 Children should feel   _____

a her son ride a motorbike.

b over kids all the time or they'll never become independent.

c complicated now than it used to be for our grandparents.

d free to say what they are thinking.

e difficulty in life and we should try to learn from it.

f manners, for example always saying 'thank you'.

g yourselves for half an hour?

h into trouble when I was young.

5 **Match words 1–8 with definitions a–h.**

1 arrangement   2 authority   3 complicated

4 difficulty   5 entertain   6 force

7 independent   8 ~~manners~~

a the way you behave   _8_

b a plan to make something happen   _____

c when you have control over others   _____

d when you don't need help from other people   _____

e to make someone do something they don't want to do   _____

f difficult to understand   _____

g a problem   _____

h to do something funny or that interests people   _____

Functional language
End conversations politely

1 Choose the correct alternatives.

A: Hi Charis! Long time, no see. How are you?

B: I'm really well, thanks, and you?

A: Yeah, I'm fine. Busy, as usual!

B: Tell me about it! **1** *Listen*/*Listening*, I'm really sorry, but I've **2** *get*/*got* to go. I'm **3** *actual*/*actually* in a rush.

A: Oh, OK. No worries.

B: My bus is about **4** *to leave*/*leaving*. But it's **5** *been*/*being* great seeing you.

A: Yeah, good to see you, too.

B: Sorry to rush **6** *on*/*off* like this. It'd be great to catch **7** *up*/*on* some time soon.

A: Sure. How about next week?

B: Yes, good idea. I'll call you tomorrow. Sorry, I've got to **8** *run*/*running*. Bye!

A: See you!

2 Put the words in the correct order to make sentences.

A: In the evening, we went to that new Italian restaurant in town and we had the best pasta I've ever eaten.

B: interrupt, / to / need / going / Sorry / get / but / I

1 *Sorry to interrupt, but I need to get going.*

A: Oh, OK.

B: a / at / I've / class / 6.30 / got

2 _____

A: It's fine!

B: train / leave / is / My / to / about

3 _____

A: Don't worry!

B: great / was / catch up / to / It

4 _____

A: Yes, it was great to see you, too.

B: rush / this / Sorry / off / to / like

5 _____

A: It's fine, really.

B: rest / your / Enjoy / of / evening / the

6 _____ !

A: You too.

B: soon / See / you

7 _____

Listening

1 🔊 **2.01 Listen to a meeting for new employees. Which things does Camilla <u>not</u> mention?**

a clothes   **b** health and safety   **c** illness   **d** money
e working hours   **f** the union

2 Listen again and answer the questions.

1 What sort of meeting is taking place?

_____

2 Is the meeting formal or informal?

_____

3 Who is Camilla?

_____

4 Who is George?

_____

5 Which floor is Camilla's office on?

_____

3 Listen again and complete George's notes.

> Health and **1** _safety_ rules
> - If there's a **2** _____ , don't use lift
> - Use stairs and meet in **3** _____
> - Each **4** _____ meets in special place – look on map to find out where
>
> **5** _____ courses
> - Let Camilla know if interested.
> - At least two people/department must do course
> - **6** _____ contact details on company website
> - **7** _____ policy on clothes – **8** _____ clothes all the time
> - Company has flexible working hours, e.g. changing **9** _____ or taking time off
> - **10** _____ times – speak to manager about them, probably flexible

Reading

1 Read the article and choose the best summary.

You should practise …

a a lot to learn a new skill.

b in exactly the same way every time to learn a new skill.

c in a slightly different way each time to learn a new skill.

2 Read again and match questions a–e with paragraphs 1–5.

a Why are the results of the experiment interesting? ___3___

b What have scientists discovered and how did they show it was true? _____

c How do we usually learn a new skill? _____

d What might these results mean for the future? _____

e How we can use this in our own learning? _____

3 Read the email and choose the correct alternatives.

Hi Julia,

I'm sending you a link to a really interesting ¹*article*/letter about the best way to practise new things. You know how you're always telling me that practice makes perfect. Well, it's ²*true*/false, in a way! A recent ³*TV programme*/report has shown that you should practise slightly differently each time because this helps you to learn more ⁴*quickly*/easily. The ⁵*difference must be big*/mustn't be too big. I decided to try this out with my guitar practice last week and it works! I learnt a piece of music more ⁶*quickly*/slowly than I normally do!

Speak soon!

Love,
Clara

Does practice really make perfect?

1 Have you ever heard the old phrase, 'Practice makes perfect'? Whether we're learning how to dance, play a new instrument or developing our technique at a new sport, we usually just repeat the same action again and again until we can do it. My teachers always used to tell me that the more I practised, the more highly skilled I would become at any activity. In 2008, author Malcolm Gladwell wrote about 'the 10,000-hour rule'. This said that if you want to become an expert at a skill, you must practise it for 10,000 hours. However, a recent report by scientists at John Hopkins University has shown that the key to learning a new skill isn't how much time you spend practising, but the <u>way</u> in which you practise.

2 The scientists found that we learn more quickly if we slightly change the way we practise an activity each time we do it. To prove this, they carried out an experiment by teaching 86 people a new skill – how to control a computer with a new type of mouse. The researchers divided the people into three groups and each group had a session of 45 minutes to practise the new skill.

Six hours later, the first group repeated the same exercise again in exactly the same way, the second group practised it in a slightly different way and the third group didn't practise again. At the end, the scientists tested everyone's ability to do the skill. It was no surprise that the third group got the worst results in the tests. What was surprising was that the second group did <u>twice</u> as well as the first group.

3 These results are useful because they help us to understand how our brains remember information and learn new things. By changing our practice slightly, our brains have to work harder. Pablo A Celnik, the scientist who led this research, said that the differences between practices must be small, for example changing the size or weight of a tennis ball or racket. If the differences are too big, then there will be no improvement in learning speed.

4 These results are not only important for those of us who are learning new leisure skills, they might also help people who have been in an accident. For example, sometimes people have to learn to walk or talk again, and this technique can help them to do these things faster. Celnik says that more research still needs to be done, but that this could help patients recover more quickly.

5 So, the old phrase 'Practice makes perfect' isn't exactly wrong. You must practise to become perfect at a new skill. But just remember that changing the way you practise each time will give you better results!

4 Read the article again. Choose the correct option a, b or c.

1 Malcolm Gladwell says that …
   a some people can never become an expert, no matter how much they practise.
   b you can become an expert in any skill if you practise it for 10,000 hours.
   c the way you practise is more important than how long you practise.

2 Scientists have discovered that you learn more quickly if you practise …
   a in the same way each time.
   b in a slightly different way each time.
   c in a completely different way each time.

3 They proved this by carrying out an experiment with a group of …
   a 86 people, who they divided into three groups.
   b 86 people, who they divided into two groups.
   c 45 people, who they divided into six groups.

4 The group that did worst in the test …
   a practised in the same way twice.
   b practised slightly differently the second time.
   c only practised once.

5 The people who practised in the same way twice did … as well in the test as those people who practised again in a slightly different way.
   a half   b just   c twice

6 Pablo A Celnik explained that the difference between practise sessions …
   a must only be small.   b must be large.   c doesn't matter.

7 This discovery could mean that people who are learning to walk and talk again …
   a won't need these skills anymore.
   b can learn faster.
   c will end up being able to walk and talk better.

8 The writer now thinks that the phrase, 'Practice makes perfect' …
   a isn't right at all.
   b is completely right.
   c is partly right.

5 Read the article again. Answer the questions.

1 What does the phrase 'practice makes perfect' mean?
   Repeat an action again and again until you can do it.

2 What advice did the writer's teachers give him?

3 In what year did Malcolm Gladwell write a book about practising a skill?

4 What did scientists ask 86 people to do in the experiment?

5 What was surprising about the results of the second group?

6 What do these results help us to understand about the brain?

7 Who is Pablo A Celnik?

8 What sort of people could this research help?

6 Find words in the article to match definitions 1−8.

1 someone who is highly skilled at something (paragraph 1)   _expert_
2 show that something is definitely true (paragraph 2)
3 a period of time for an activity (paragraph 2)
4 the study and discovery of new information about something (paragraph 3)
5 when something gets better (paragraph 3)
6 the time when you aren't working (paragraph 4)
7 a particular way of doing an activity (paragraph 4)
8 become well again after illness (paragraph 4)

Writing

1 **Read the emails and choose the correct alternatives.**

These are ¹*formal/informal* emails to a ²*friend/stranger*. They contain ³*news/hotel reservations*.

1 Hi Marta,

Long time, no see! Hope you're well. How are things with you?

We've just come back from holiday. We spent two weeks in Croatia – it was so relaxing! We were staying in a lovely hotel near Dubrovnik. The landscape was stunning! We went for long walks and ate lots of delicious food.

It was a good holiday because there was something for everyone. I was happy because I managed to finish three whole books! Jaber was happy because he got to go running every day. He woke up every morning at 6 a.m. so that he could go for a run along the beach before breakfast! Can you believe that? Also, the kids were happy because they enjoyed the water sports, though I think they got a bit bored by the end. Maybe we'll go back there one day. Who knows?

Have you been away yet this summer? Let's get a date in the diary for lunch or dinner soon.

Best wishes,

Layla

2 Hi Marta,

It was lovely to get your email and hear all your news. Congratulations on winning that business award – you must be thrilled! I can't believe your company is only three years old and you're already winning awards! That's so cool!

Everything's OK at this end. Dominic is well and has just had a promotion at work. The kids are fine, but I can never get Tom off his phone! What's the matter with kids today?

Things are a bit difficult for me at work right now. The company has been struggling for a while. We're about to be taken over by Kliemens and Sons, so I think that some people will be made redundant. I'm going to start looking for a new job, though I don't really want to leave. I might see if there are any jobs at Martins Harris because I heard that they're expanding. Have you ever done any work for them?

Anyway, better get on. Speak soon.

Love,

Valerie

2 **Read the emails again. Are the statements below true (T) or false (F)?**

Email 1

1 Marta and Layla have met up with each other recently.   *F*
2 Layla is going on holiday to Croatia next week.   ....
3 Layla likes reading.   ....
4 Jaber loves running, but he didn't run when he was on holiday.   ....
5 Layla's children were really bored for the whole holiday.   ....
6 Layla and Marta might meet soon.   ....

Email 2

7 Valerie's company has recently won a business award.   ....
8 Dominic is doing well at work.   ....
9 Tom doesn't have a phone.   ....
10 Valerie's company was taken over last month by Kliemens and Sons.   ....
11 She thinks she might lose her job.   ....
12 She thinks that Martins Harris might be increasing in size.   ....

2

3 Read the Focus box. Then answer the questions in Exercise 4.

///////////////////////////////////////

Linking words and questions in informal emails

Informal emails and letters are often more like a conversation. You tend to use short sentences and simple linking words like *and, so, but, though, because*. You might just use a dash to show a connection or to make clear that information is not central to understanding the rest of the sentence. You also often include questions as if you are talking to someone face to face. Sometimes these questions will be rhetorical, i.e. they don't require an answer.

4 In Emails 1 and 2, underline examples of:
1 expressions that we use in spoken English
2 short sentences
3 linking words: *and, so, but, though* and *because*
4 dashes
5 real questions
6 rhetorical questions

5 Choose the correct option a, b or c.
1 Today is my first day in my new job, __c__ I feel a bit nervous.
2 The business is struggling a bit, _____ it's going to be fine.
3 Mei left her last job _____ her boss was bullying her.
4 I've had a promotion _____ I've also had a pay rise.
5 He's looking for a new job, _____ he hasn't been made redundant yet.
6 I missed my train, _____ I was late for work.
7 He was made redundant _____ his role wasn't needed any more.
8 He was given an interview, _____ he didn't get the job.

1	a but	b because	c so
2	a so	b but	c because
3	a but	b because	c though
4	a and	b though	c but
5	a because	b so	c though
6	a though	b so	c because
7	a because	b but	c though
8	a because	b but	c so

6 Match the sentence halves.
1 Work is really busy at the moment _____
2 Sam has been promoted _____
3 We were on holiday last week _____
4 I wasn't at work yesterday _____
5 Marie had an audition for a new play _____
6 My mother has moved house _____
7 I've decided to take up a new hobby _____
8 Let's meet up soon _____

a but unfortunately she didn't get the part.
b and she's living near us now.
c though I don't know what to try.
d and he's now Head of Internal Affairs.
e because I haven't seen you for months!
f and the weather in Spain was amazing!
g because I've just started a big, new project.
h so I didn't pick up your email.

7 Read the questions. Are they real questions (R) or rhetorical questions (Rh)?
1 What does it matter? _____
2 Have you seen that film yet? _____
3 Who cares? _____
4 What's the point? _____
5 What's that man's name? _____
6 Whose coat is this? _____
7 Why you need it? _____
8 Is it really worth it? _____

Prepare

8 Choose one of these tasks.
a Write an email to a friend, telling them news about a holiday you've been on recently.
b Imagine you are Marta and reply to Layla's email.

9 Before you write, make notes about these points:
• the holiday you want to write about
• questions you want to ask and answer in your email
• how you will start and end your email

Write

10 Write your email. Use your notes from Exercise 9 and the Focus box to help you.

Vocabulary
Tourist places

1 **Match words 1–8 with definitions a–h.**

1 cave   2 cliff   3 ~~fort~~

4 nature reserve   5 remains

6 temple   7 tour   8 view

a a stong building that was built to protect people   *3*

b the parts of a place that are left after most of it has gone   ......

c a high area of land close to the sea   ......

d what you can see from a certain place   ......

e a building where people go to pray   ......

f a large hole in the side of a hill or mountain or under the ground   ......

g a natural area where plants and animals are safe   ......

h a trip around a place or area   ......

2 **Complete the sentences using the words in the box.**

cliff   climb   medieval   nature reserve
restored   steep   ~~tour~~   view

1 We're going on a ....*tour*.... of the castle, so we'll see all the important parts.

2 Many tourists visit the remains of this .... fort, which was built in 1300 CE.

3 This recently .... temple looks just like it did when it was first built.

4 This mountain rises very quickly, so it's very .... to climb.

5 I've heard that there's an amazing .... from the 20th floor. Shall we go up there?

6 Shall we .... to the top of the hill or shall we drive?

7 We can do a tour of the .... and see lots of interesting animals.

8 They stood near the edge of the .... and looked down at the sea.

Grammar
Present perfect simple questions and answers

3 **Put the words in the correct order to make questions and answers.**

1 **A:** been / you / Have / France / ever / to?
   Have you ever been to France?
   B: four / been / times. / Yes, / I've
   ....

2 **A:** the / you / ancient temple / Have / been / to / ever?
   ....
   B: haven't, / I'd / No, / sometime / to / but / I / love / go
   ....

3 **A:** you / hot springs / visited / Have / the?
   ....
   B: thinking / tomorrow / No, / I'm / of / but / going
   ....

4 **A:** coal mine / looked around / you / Have / the?
   ....
   B: supposed / very interesting / No, / it's / but / be / to
   ....

5 **A:** that / yet / steep mountain / you / Have / climbed?
   ....
   B: going / it / No, / I'm / do / to / tomorrow / but
   ....

4 **Find and correct eight mistakes in the conversation.**

Have you ever been
A: ~~Did you ever go~~ to Italy?

B: Yeah, I been three times.

A: Oh, OK. Have you ever visit Rome?

B: Yeah, I spent three weeks there last August. I've done a tour around the city while I was there. It's been amazing there.

A: Did you go to Granada last summer?

B: No, but it's supposing to be wonderful. I'm love to go sometime.

A: I'm thinking for going next year. I'm going to book it this weekend!

3B

Vocabulary
Science and research

1 Choose the correct alternatives.

There has been lot of ¹*research*/*risk* to find out what ²*explores*/*causes* cancer and why some cancer ³*genes*/*cells* grow more quickly than others. Governments have ⁴*predicted*/*invested* billions in trying to find a ⁵*cure*/*change* for the disease. Scientists have also ⁶*explored*/*affected* ways to find out who is most at ⁷*rate*/*risk* of getting cancer by identifying specific ⁸*genes*/*cures*.

2 Choose the correct option a, b or c.

1 All of the world has been affected _____ climate change.
   a on   **b** to   **c** by

2 We're worried that there's a real risk _____ fire.
   a to   **b** on   **c** of

3 Soon we will run out _____ oil and gas.
   a of   **b** on   **c** in

4 We need to invest more money _____ research.
   a to   **b** in   **c** about

5 We're exploring different sources _____ energy that we can use.
   a to   **b** for   **c** of

6 We're developing a cure _____ Alzheimer's.
   a for   **b** on   **c** in

3 Complete the sentences with the words and phrases in the box.

> earthquake   fallen steadily   global birth rate
> identifying genes   increased dramatically   predict
> solar power

1 Scientists have done a lot of research into
   ___*identifying genes*___ that cause cancer.

2 _____ is good for the planet because it uses energy from the sun, which will never run out.

3 The _____ tells us how many babies are born each year.

4 An _____ happens when rock under the Earth moves suddenly.

5 The price of oil has gone up very quickly. It has _____ since January.

6 There has been a regular decrease in the price of gas. It has _____ since January.

7 Scientists can't _____ when we will be affected by drought.

Grammar
Present perfect simple and continuous

4 Choose the correct option, a or b.

1 Tom started studying two hours ago. He's still studying and he's on chapter four of his textbook.
   a Tom *has studied*/*has been studying* for two hours.
   b Tom *has read*/*has been reading* three chapters of his text book.

2 After finishing university, Rachel and Hassan started doing research into the causes of global warming. They are still doing their research.
   a Rachel and Hassan *have done*/*have been doing* research together since they left university.
   b Rachel and Hassan *have won*/*have been winning* several prizes for their research.

3 Lisa is a scientist who started researching earthquakes 18 years ago. She correctly predicted earthquakes which happened in 2004, 2011 and 2017.
   a Lisa *has predicted*/*has been predicting* three earthquakes.
   b Lisa *has researched*/*has been researching* earthquakesfor 18 years.

4 Marta works for a company that invests in solar power. She is travelling around the world at the moment. She began her trip eight months ago.
   a Marta *has travelled*/*has been travelling* for eight months.
   b Marta *has visited*/*has been visiting* 12 solar power stations so far.

5 Complete the sentences. Use the present perfect simple or continuous form of the verbs in brackets.

1 I *'ve read* (read) that book you gave me. I finished it this morning.

2 I _____ (read) this book for four weeks and I've still got another 100 pages to read!

3 There _____ (be) three earthquakes on this island in the last year.

4 Scientists _____ (look) for a cure for cancer for many years.

5 Scientists _____ (agree) that there's a link between some genes and cancer.

6 We _____ (know) for ages that pollution is linked to climate change.

7 How long _____ (he / play) that video game?

8 How many books _____ (the author / write)?

9 I _____ (work) on my essay all day and I'm only halfway through it.

10 How much _____ (scientists / discover) about this gene.

Grammar
Obligation and permission

1 Choose the correct option a, b or c.

1 You _a_ buy a ticket before you get on the train or you might get a fine.

 a must   **b** mustn't   **c** don't have to

2 You _____ wait outside. You can come in.

 a must   **b** mustn't   **c** don't have to

3 You can wear your shoes in the house. You _____ take them off.

 a must   **b** mustn't   **c** needn't

4 If you want access to healthcare, then you _____ register with a doctor.

 a have to   **b** needn't   **c** can't

5 You _____ use your phone during a film at the cinema because it disturbs other people.

 a don't have to   **b** shouldn't   **c** needn't

6 We _____ park here. That sign says that parking is for employees only and we don't work here!

 a can   **b** can't   **c** must

2 Read the rules, then complete the sentences below using the correct form of *be* and structures in the box.

> allowed to   not allowed to   ~~required to~~
> not required to   supposed to   not supposed to

Student accommodation rules

1 You <u>must</u> pay your rent in full every month.

 You _____ _required to_ _____ pay your rent in full every month.

2 You <u>can</u> delay your payment by a few days if you need to.

 You _____ delay your payment by a few days if you need to.

3 You <u>should</u> let the office know if you're going to be away for more than three nights.

 You _____ let the office know if you're going to be away for more than three nights.

4 You <u>don't have to</u> tell them if you're away for less than three nights.

 You _____ tell them if you're away for less than three nights.

5 You <u>shouldn't</u> play your music too loud.

 You _____ play your music too loud.

6 You <u>can't</u> have more than eight people in your room at any time.

 You _____ have more than eight people in your room at any time.

Vocabulary
Rules and customs

3 Match the sentence halves.

1 You should let people   _g_

2 There's no charge   _____

3 It's not polite to swear   _____

4 Everyone can access   _____

5 Let's split   _____

6 Please could you respect   _____

7 Thanks! I'll buy the next drink in   _____

8 If you drop rubbish, you'll have to pay   _____

a health care when they need it.

b return.

c in public.

d my personal space?

e a fine.

f for using this ferry.

g off the bus before you get on.

h the bill for the meal.

4 Match words 1–8 with definitions a–h.

1 access   2 ~~bill~~   3 fine   4 personal space

5 privacy   6 respect   7 split   8 swear

a a document that shows how much you have to pay for something   _2_

b the right to live without other people knowing about your life   _____

c use bad language   _____

d to share something between two or more people   _____

e money you have to pay when you do something that's against the law   _____

f the area around someone's body   _____

g the right to go somewhere or use something   _____

h show care and politeness to someone or something   _____

5 Complete the sentences with the missing words.

1 You shouldn't s_____ because bad language can upset people.

2 If you drive too fast, you might have to pay a f_____ .

3 It's important to show r_____ to people who are older than us.

4 Some people have to travel a long way to a _____ health care.

5 The friends decided to split the b_____ equally between them.

6 Sara asked everyone to leave her alone and respect her p_____ .

7 If somebody buys you something, you should buy them something in r_____ .

8 There isn't usually a c_____ for tap water in restaurants.

Functional language

Ask for and give explanations

1 Complete the conversation with the words in the box.

> call exactly for heard kind
> mean stand ~~what~~

1

A: Have you tried cooking with orzo?

B: Orzo? I don't think so, I don't know
¹ _____what_____ that is.

A: It's a ² _____ of pasta. You should try it, it's delicious.

2

A: I'd like to try to play … umm … I'm not sure what you'd ³ _____ it in English. It's a bit like tennis, but you hit the ball against a wall.

B: Oh, I know what you ⁴ _____ . It's called squash.

3

A: I'm thinking of donating to the RSPCA.

B: I haven't ⁵ _____ of that before. What does it ⁶ _____ for?

A: The Royal Society for the Prevention of Cruelty to Animals.

B: Ah, I see.

4

A: My friend asked me if I have a corkscrew. What is it ⁷ _____ ?

B: It's a thing ⁸ _____ opening bottles of wine.

2 Match the sentence halves.

1 I don't know   _g_
2 What is   _____
3 I'm not sure what   _____
4 I'm not sure how   _____
5 It's a bit   _____
6 It stands   _____
7 Do you know   _____
8 Yeah, I've   _____

a you'd call it in English.
b what I mean?
c like chicken.
d for Common Era.
e to explain it.
f got it now.
g what that is, I'm afraid.
h it exactly?

Listening

1 🔊 **3.01 Listen to the conversation. What is it about?**

  a Two friends are talking about holidays.

  b Two people are visiting a travel agency to plan a holiday.

  c Two work colleagues are talking about business trips.

2 Listen again. Are these sentences true (T) or false (F)?

  1 Zara has been to the north of Africa, but has never been to South Africa.   _T_

  2 Patrick worked in a gold mine in South Africa when he was a student.   _____

  3 Zara visited a gold mine last summer.   _____

  4 The Castle of Good Hope is one of the oldest buildings in South Africa.   _____

  5 Patrick already knows where he wants to go on holiday this year.   _____

  6 Jess doesn't like spending all day at the beach.   _____

  7 Patrick has visited an ancient temple before.   _____

  8 Zara loves Indonesian food.   _____

3 Listen again and choose the correct alternatives.

  1 Zara has been to Morocco _four_/_five_ times.

  2 Patrick lived in South Africa for _two_/_three_ months when he was younger.

  3 You have to drive for _15_/_40_ minutes to get to the Kromdraai Gold Mine from Johannesburg.

  4 The Castle of Good Hope was built in the _16th_/_17th_ century.

  5 The flight between Johannesburg and Cape Town takes about _two_/_four_ hours.

  6 Patrick is going to go on holiday for _two_/_three_ weeks in August.

  7 Zara went to Indonesia _three_/_four_ years ago.

  8 Some of the temples in Bali are _hundreds_/_thousands_ of years old.

YOUNG SCIENTISTS

Reading

1 Read the article. What is it about?

2 Read the article again. Are the sentences true (T) or false (F).

1 Jack started his research in the basement of his house. ....

2 A cancer expert called Aniran Maitra was very interested in Jack's ideas. ....

3 Jack couldn't work on his research at the weekends. ....

4 Jack failed to complete his research. ....

5 Sara discovered a new type of plant. ....

6 Sara Volz created a laboratory in her kitchen. ....

7 Sara is at university now. ....

8 Sara's experiments don't always work. ....

3 Read the article again and answer the questions about each scientist.

Jack Andraka

1 What did he discover?
He discovered a new test for a particular type of cancer cell.

2 How old was he at the time of the discovery?

3 Why was the discovery important?

4 Where did he win a prize?

Sara Volz

5 What did she discover?

6 How old was she at the time of the discovery?

7 Why was the discovery important?

8 What prize did she win?

1 Over the years, some of the most important scientific discoveries have come from the minds of young people. Isaac Newton and Albert Einstein both started their research when they were teenagers. So what are young scientists working on these days?

2 Jack Andraka was only 15 years old when he found a new test for a particular type of cancer cell. He started doing his research in a school laboratory and later continued it from the basement of his house. Cancer expert, Aniran Maitra found out about Jack's work and was very impressed with his ideas. He invited Jack to work in the laboratory at a local university and helped him with his training.

3 Jack worked on his research over seven months. He worked after school, at weekends and during the holidays. He even spent his 15th birthday in the laboratory! Finally, he developed a new test for cancer which is less expensive and more likely to find cancer cells than any other tests which have been used. Experts have said that this is a very important development in cancer research. Jack won a prize for his discovery at the Intel International Science and Engineering Fair. Since then, he has spoken at several conferences and he has started his own company. He didn't want to leave high school, though, because he enjoyed it.

4 Jack Andraka is not the only young scientist who has been making discoveries. Sara Volz was 17 years old when she decided to develop a fuel using plants that she grew in her bedroom. She created her own laboratory and developed the new fuel under her bed. The plants needed light at certain times of day and Sara slept in the same light cycle as her plants. Her discovery is important because it shows how in the future plants could be used as fuel instead of oil or gas. She won the Intel Science Talent Search prize for her discovery.

5 Since then, Sara has been studying at university and she works in a laboratory, too. She thinks that it's exciting to question the world. She has been working with other scientists to identify genes and to change them in a way that might cure some diseases. She said that experiments aren't always successful. She believes that failure can be good because when an experiment fails, you learn something new.

4 Which of the people do the statements refer to? Choose an option, Jack (J), Sara (S) or both (B).

1 The person made an important discovery. _B_

2 The person started their research in one place, but then moved to another. _____

3 The person changed their lifestyle while they were doing research. _____

4 The person's discovery may help to save money. _____

5 The person's discovery may help the environment. _____

6 The person has spoken in front of groups of people. _____

7 The person's research may help cure diseases. _____

8 The person didn't want to give something up. _____

9 The person recognises that you can learn a lot when things don't work, as well as when they do. _____

10 The person ignored a special day to focus on their work. _____

5 Match words 1–7 from the article with definitions a–g.

1 conference   2 cycle   3 discovery
4 experiment   5 failure
6 laboratory   7 particular

a something that you find out _____ (paragraph 1)

b relating to one specific thing rather thananother similar ones _____ (paragraph 2)

c the place where scientists carry out experiments _____ (paragraph 2)

d a long meeting about a particular topic _____ (paragraph 3)

e a set of events that happens again and again _____ (paragraph 4)

f something that is not a success _____ (paragraph 5)

g a scientific test _____ (paragraph 5)

6 Read and complete the text with sentences a–d.

Can plants really replace oil and gas?

The world is running out of oil and gas. **1** _____ . Perhaps fuels made from plants could be the answer.

Fuels from plants, however, are renewable, which means they won't run out in the future. **2** _____ .

However, fuels from plants are not as efficient as oil and gas. **3** _____ . Also, making these plant fuels uses a lot of water and energy at the moment.

4 _____ . However, with the right research and development, they could become an important alternative in the future.

a This means we need more plants to produce the same amount of energy.

b These fossil fuels are non-renewable, which means once they have been used up, we can't create any more of them.

c Plants fuels might not be the answer to our energy problems just yet.

d They also help the environment because they don't produce as much pollution as oil and gas when burnt.

7 Which scientist's discovery from the first reading relates to this text?

8 Write two advantages and two disadvantages of fuels made from plants.
Advantages:
1 _____
2 _____

Disadvantages:
1 _____
2 _____

Writing

1 Read the two summaries.

Which of them:

a describes a benefit of being away from your own country?

b describes a new way that people are trying to make a difference?

Think global, go global! is a magazine article by Martin Peterson. He <u>argues</u> that business is global, so studying and living abroad is the only way to become a global leader. He gives the example of an American company, BCE Electronics, which failed to take over another business because the CEO didn't understand the way South American people do business. Peterson discusses why some students study in their home country and claims that many American degrees don't offer an international part of their course. He goes on to say that many people can't afford to study abroad and talks about scholarships. He lists the advantages studying abroad can bring: understanding different cultures, learning how to listen to others and becoming more confident. He ends with the words of an American student who studied in Brazil. The student explains how being a foreigner gives you new ideas because you have to think about things in different ways.

Young people using social media for change is a newspaper article by Bella Hanbury. She explains that young people are using social media to push for change and discusses how they use social platforms to get together for a shared cause. She gives the example of the #MeToo movement and lists protests and marches that have been organised via social media. She goes on to talk about gender differences. She claims that young women are twice as likely to use social media as a way of campaigning on issues and talks about the fact that young men are twice as likely to use it to communicate with politicians. She ends with the results of a report on the impact of online social media and argues that social platforms should recognise the power that they have and make sure that their services are accessible for all.

2 Read the texts again. Are the sentences true (T) or false (F)?

Summary 1

1 The writer thinks that you can become a global leader without travelling abroad.

2 According to the writer, many American courses have an international element.

3 A lot of people don't have enough money to study abroad.

Summary 2

4 The writer thinks that young people use social media to make positive changes.

5 According to the writer, there is little difference in the way young men and women use social media.

6 The writer thinks that social media should be more accessible.

3a Read Summary 1 again. Tick (✓) the information that is given in the summary.

1 who wrote the article ✓
2 what other articles it is similar to
3 where the article is from
4 the main point of the article
5 how the person writing the summary feels about the article
6 examples/extra details
7 how the article ends
8 other articles it might be interesting to read

b Read Summary 2 again. Put the information from the summary in the correct order.

a the main point of the article _____
b another point that the article makes _____
c the first or main example the author uses to explain the point _____
d how the article ends _____
e the title of the article, the name of the author, and where it comes from ___1___

4 Read the Focus box and check your answers to Exercise 3.

Writing a summary

When you write a short summary of an article, use this structure:
1 Say who the article is by, what it's called and where it's from.
2 Give the overall point/argument/theory the article puts forward.
3 Give the first or main example the author uses to explain the point.
4 Give one or two more details about the example or introduce another point that the article makes.
5 Explain how the article ends.

A summary doesn't always follow the same pattern as the original article, because an article often starts with an example or background information, and the main point the author is making may only become clear later in the article.

As well as thinking about the structure, remember that:
• when you summarise, you need to paraphrase (i.e. explain ideas in your own words, rather than copy from the article).
• it's a good idea to take notes on the key ideas/ examples from each paragraph of the original article while you're reading. This will help you structure your summary.
• there are useful summarising verbs and phrases you can use, e.g. *claim, goes on to (discuss)*, etc.

5 Underline eight summarising verbs or phrases in the summaries. The first one is done for you as an example.

6 Choose the correct alternatives.

1 The writer *claims/explains* how global temperatures have increased.
2 He *goes on to say that/talks about* solar power and other sources of energy.
3 She *lists/argues* the possible causes of global warming.
4 He *discusses/ends by saying that* the choices that voters had on that day.
5 She *claims/lists* that the president already knew the truth.
6 He *emphasises the fact that/ends with* his own opinion.
7 She *goes on to say/lists* that many people disagree with this.
8 He *gives the example of/argues that* there's no future for the company.
9 She *emphasises the fact/talks about* that not everybody is choosing this way of paying for things.
10 She *gives the example/lists* the benefits of travelling abroad.

Prepare

7a You're going to summarise an article. Choose whether you want to summarise:
• the article about young scientists on page 22
• another article from a newspaper or magazine

b Make notes about the key ideas from each paragraph of the article you are going to summarise.

Write

8 Write your summary. Use your notes from Exercise 7 and the Focus box to help you.

Grammar
Past simple and past continuous

1 Choose the correct option a or b.

1 I was bending down to pick something up …
   a when the woman knocked me over.
   b when the woman was knocking me over.

2 We were waiting for the taxi …
   a when the car accident happened.
   b when the car accident was happening.

3 When it was raining …
   a I accidentally dropped my bus ticket in a pool of water.
   b I was accidentally dropping my bus ticket in a pool of water.

4 Jai fell off the ladder …
   a while he washed the windows.
   b while he was washing the windows.

5 I didn't realise …
   a that he listened to me on speaker phone.
   b that he was listening to me on speaker phone.

6 We were at the airport …
   a when Jack realised that he'd forgotten his passport.
   b when Jack was realising that he'd forgotten his passport.

7 How did Bea manage to hurt her toe …
   a while she washed her hair?
   b while she was washing her hair?

8 I hurt my leg …
   a when I fell over.
   b when I was falling over.

2 Find and correct five mistakes in sentences 1–8.

   was looking
1 Jane ~~looked~~ in her bag when she walked into the streetlight.

2 Kim opened the door of the washing machine and flooded the kitchen.

3 Ellie accidentally was picking up another woman's bag because she thought it was her bag.

4 I was talking on the phone when I was smelling the pizza burning in the oven.

5 As I was lighting the barbecue, my hair was catching fire.

6 It took several months to repair all the damage from the flood.

7 I tried an expensive perfume in a shop when my phone rang and the bottle slipped out of my hand.

8 My neighbour was fixing his roof when he slipped and fell off his ladder.

3 Complete the text with the correct form of the verbs in brackets.

I had a really embarrassing experience yesterday. I **1**_____ (be) in the shopping centre and I **2**_____ (hurry) up the escalator, when I passed a woman who **3**_____ (look) in her bag for something. Somehow my jumper **4**_____ (get) caught on the zip on the woman's bag. I nearly **5**_____ (slip) and **6**_____ (fell) back down the escalator. I couldn't free my jumper from the zip on her bag. The woman and her friend **7**_____ (try) to help me, but they couldn't. So we **8**_____ (have to) travel up the escalator together!

Vocabulary
Accidents and mistakes

4 Complete the missing words in the sentences.

1 The glass s_____ out of Henri's hand and smashed on the floor.

2 Felix left the taps on and f_____ the bathroom.

3 The waitress s_____ the soup all over Izzy.

4 When the kitchen c_____ fire, I was worried that the whole house was going to burn down.

5 Thomas accidentally k_____ over his grandmother's expensive vase.

6 Fiona c_____ her motorcycle into a tree.

7 Pamela m_____ the window wrong so the curtains didn't fit.

8 I t_____ off the lights before I left, but forgot about the cooker!

5 Choose the correct option a, b or c.

1 The candle fell over and the carpet __c__ .
   a flooded   b mixed up   c caught fire

2 When the tree fell on the house, it _____ .
   a caused a lot of damage   b slipped   c checked

3 I _____ on the gas by mistake.
   a left   b slipped   c fell down

4 Ollie _____ some chemicals on his hand by mistake.
   a spilt   b measured   c slipped

5 During the storm, the rain _____ the school.
   a turned off   b flooded   c pressed

6 Kate _____ the cooker.
   a didn't turn off   b didn't flood   c didn't charge

4B

Vocabulary
Crime in the news

1 Match words 1–8 with definitions a–h.

1 criminal   2 gang   3 jail   4 threat

5 trial   6 theft   7 victim   8 ~~witness~~

a   a person who sees a crime happen   _8_

b   a person who suffers from a crime   ____

c   a person who has committed a crime   ____

d   a place where people who have committed crimes are sent as a punishment   ____

e   the crime of taking something that does not belong to you   ____

f   a group of people who work together to commit crimes   ____

g   a statement that tells someone that you will do something bad to them if they don't do what they want   ____

h   a formal meeting in a court of law where people decide if a person has committed a crime or no   ____

2 Complete the sentences using the pairs of words in the box.

| arrested/get away   attack/victim   ~~broke into/gang~~ |
| theft/claimed   freed/trial   witness/victim |

1 The __gang broke into__ the store at night.

2 The police _____ the criminals while they were trying to _____ .

3 The _____ saw the criminal attack the _____ .

4 After the _____ at the shop, the owner _____ £50,000 from her insurance.

5 The _____ took place while the _____ was walking home.

6 There wasn't enough evidence for a _____ , so they _____ the man.

3 Complete the sentences with the words from the box.

| attack   claimed   freed   jail   ~~reported~~   trap |
| victim   worth |

1 The witness _reported_ the crime to the police.

2 The criminal got out of _____ after three years.

3 My neighbour's camera was stolen and he _____ £300 from his insurance company.

4 The police set a _____ to catch thieves.

5 After 15 years, they _____ gang leader from prison.

6 Robbers have stolen a horse _____ over half a million pounds.

7 There has been a serious cyber _____ on the computers of a major bank.

8 The _____ of the crime is recovering in hospital as she was quite badly hurt in the attack.

Grammar
Past perfect simple

4 Choose the correct alternatives.

1 He *was/'d been* in prison for seven years when I *met/'d met* him.

2 We *realised/'d realised* that the thief *got in/had got in* through the back door.

3 Paul *remembered/had remembered* that he *already closed/had already closed* the window.

4 We *were/'d been* in the house for 20 minutes before we *realised/'d realised* the robber was still there!

5 I *never heard/'d never heard* of the gang before I *read/had read* the newspaper.

6 I *was/had been* on the plane when I remembered I *left/'d left* the key in the door.

5 Complete the sentences with the past perfect simple form of the verb in brackets and one of the words or phrases in the box.

| after   already   because   before   ~~by the time~~ |
| until (x2)   when |

1 The gang _had disappeared by the time_ the police arrived. (disappear)

2 The woman got away in a blue car _____ she _____ the garage. (rob)

3 Laura was terrified because she _____ the victim of a crime _____ . (never be)

4 Ava didn't realise someone _____ her phone _____ she got home. (steal)

5 She was on the train _____ she remembered that she _____ the door. (not lock)

6 The robber had to go to hospital _____ she _____ by the guard dog. (bite)

7 Nobody noticed that Sam _____ the party _____ the disco started. (leave)

8 The detectives had to get things right this time. They _____ too many mistakes. (make)

6 Choose the correct alternatives.

By the time he arrived at college, Hugo
[1]*heard/had already heard* the news, but when he saw the damage, it
[2]*was/had been* still a shock. A gang of thieves [3]*broke/had broken* into the building the night before. They [4]*stole/had stolen* lots of computers and other equipment, and then they [5]*lit/had lit* a fire. Worst still, they [6]*attacked/had attacked* the night guard, who was now in hospital, badly hurt. The police [7]*were/had been* at the college asking everyone if they [8]*saw/had seen* anyone they hadn't recognised near the building the day before. An officer [9]*asked/had asked* Hugo if he [10]*had/had had* any useful information.

Vocabulary

Complaints

1 Complete the sentences with the missing words.

1 The bank has given Justin a l_____ to help him buy his new car.

2 I can't sit on that chair because its leg is c_____ .

3 The woman in the shop couldn't s_____ o_____ the problem with my new computer.

4 We had to pay the company an extra £40 to have our new bed d_____ .

5 I can't use my phone properly because the s_____ has cracked.

6 I think I was o_____ for my new trainers because I found the same ones much cheaper online.

7 Has the hotel we're going to got free w_____ so that I can go online?

8 When I bought my new laptop, I paid extra for a three year g_____ .

2 Choose the correct alternatives.

A: Good morning, how can I help you?

B: I'd like a ¹*refund/fault* for my new bike, please.

A: May I ask what the problem is with it?

B: First, there was a ²*fault/deal* with the seat. Now the brakes have ³*turned/gone*, and it's really hard to change ⁴*gears/pedals* when I'm cycling up a hill.

A: I'm sure we can ⁵*sort/deal* out those problems for you. The bike has got a ⁶*loan/guarantee* of a year, so we can make the repairs.

B: But I'd like my money back.

A: I'm sorry, but we can't give you your money back. However, we can offer you an ⁷*overcharge/exchange*.

3 Complete the sentences with the words in the box.

back	for	off	out	~~up~~	with

1 The delivery guys turned _____*up*_____ over an hour late!

2 My laptop's broken and I'm still paying _____ the loan for it.

3 These trainers are really uncomfortable. I think I'll take them _____ .

4 I need someone to sort _____ my computer for me. It's so slow!

5 I decided to return my new watch because there was a fault _____ it.

6 The courier broke the printer, and the sales assistant tried to charge me _____ the repair!

Grammar

Reported speech

4 Choose the correct option, a or b.

1 'The screen is cracked.'
   a He said that the screen was cracked.
   b He said that the screen had cracked.

2 'I've fixed the fault.'
   a She said that she fixed the fault.
   b She said that she'd fixed the fault.

3 'You might need to take it back.'
   a He told me that I might have needed to take it back.
   b He told me that I might need to take it back.

4 'I'll pay off the loan before September.'
   a I told him that I would pay off the loan before September.
   b I told him that I paid off the loan before September.

5 'I can give you a good deal.'
   a He said that he could give me a good deal.
   b He said that he can give me a good deal.

6 'I'm sorting your bike out.'
   a The bike expert told me that he had sorted my bike out.
   b The bike expert told me that he was sorting my bike out.

7 'I'm not going to buy another pair of sunglasses from *SeeSaw*!'
   a I told the woman that I wasn't going to buy another pair of sunglasses from *SeeSaw*.
   b I told the woman that I didn't buy another pair of sunglasses from *SeeSaw*.

8 'Do you have free wifi?'
   a Caroline asked if they have free wifi.
   b Caroline asked if they had free wifi.

5 Rewrite the sentences in reported speech using the verb in brackets.

1 Greg said, 'I got a great deal on my phone.' (say)
   Greg said that he'd got a great deal on his phone.

2 'Has the engine gone?' I asked. (ask)

3 Gina said, 'You should take your tablet back and get a refund.' (tell)

4 'Can I have a discount?' she asked (ask)

5 The sales assistant said, 'Your guarantee has ended.' (explain)

6 'We'll be getting a delivery of new parts soon,' Bob said. (say)

7 'It's not your fault it broke,' said the man in the shop. (say)

8 I said, 'It's making a funny noise!' (explain)

Functional language
Respond to news

1 Put the words in the correct order to complete the conversation.

1 A: My sister has just had a baby.
   B: news / That's / wonderful
   That's wonderful news.

2 A: I'm so annoyed with myself. I don't think I did very well in my interview.
   B: you / When / hear / will?
   Oh no! _____

3 A: The doctor called today, I have to go back to the hospital for more tests.
   B: I / it / OK / goes / hope / all
   _____

4 A: Luke and I are buying a house.
   B: you're / I / really / bet / excited
   _____

5 A: I've had enough of my boss. I'm going to leave my job tomorrow.
   B: you've / you / mind / sound / like / made up / your
   Well, _____

6 A: I can't believe it! Jack says he can't go on holiday with me now and we're meant to be going next week.
   B: you're / angry / I / really / bet
   _____

7 A: The sale of the house isn't going to happen.
   B: did / When / hear / it / about / you?
   I'm sorry. _____

8 A: I've got to go now. I've got my job interview this afternoon.
   B: hope / job / you / I / get / the
   _____

2 Match statements 1–8 with responses a–h.

1 Our son passed his driving test today.   _e_
2 I've decided to leave college and get a job.   ____
3 My grandad's just been taken to hospital.   ____
4 I can't come out tonight because I've got to revise.   ____
5 My boyfriend has just left me.   ____
6 We're getting married.   ____
7 I've just been offered a fantastic job.   ____
8 I feel so ill.   ____

a Oh no! I'm sorry to hear that. I hope he's OK.
b That's annoying! Have you got much to do?
c That's amazing! Which company is it with?
d I'm sorry to hear that. Did you have an argument?
e That's great news! You must be really proud of him.
f You poor thing. Have you seen a doctor?
g You sound like you've made your mind up. Good luck with the job hunt!
h Congratulations! I hope you'll be very happy together!

Listening

1 🔊 4.01 **Listen to the conversation.**
How many of the people have been the victim of a crime?
a one   b both   c neither

2 **Listen again. Are the sentences true (T) or false (F)?**
1 Kim was walking down the high street with her friend when the crime happened.   _T_
2 The thieves were on bicycles.   ____
3 Her friend was upset because important documents from work were in the bag.   ____
4 Kim's friend didn't get her stolen items back.   ____
5 Jude believes that the crime was partly his fault.   ____
6 Jude was in France.   ____
7 The crime didn't ruin Jude's holiday.   ____
8 Jude's passport was stolen.   ____

3 **Answer the questions. Then listen and check.**
1 What did the thieves steal from Kim's friend?
_____
2 How did Kim's friend feel?
_____
3 What did Kim and her friend have to do after the crime?
_____
4 How did Jude feel about being a victim of crime?
_____
5 Where was Jude's backpack?
_____
6 How did the girl distract Jude?
_____
7 What was inside Jude's backpack?
_____
8 Why didn't Jude report the robbery to the police?
_____

Reading

1 **Read the four texts. What are they about?**
 a difficult decisions people will have to make
 b funny things that have happened to people
 c mistakes people have made

2 **Read the texts again and answer the questions.**
 1 Whose mistake involves an animal? ....
 2 Whose mistake involves transport? ....
 3 Whose mistake involves education? ....
 4 Whose mistake involves technology? ....
 5 Which two people are still trying to find solutions for their mistakes? ....
 6 Which person thinks their mistake happened because they weren't feeling well? ....
 7 Whose mistake affected the company he/she was working for? ....

1

Laila

My mistake cost me a lot of time and money. It was really inconvenient and I was very annoyed with myself. I was on a business trip in San Francisco. I had a bit of a cold and I wasn't feeling great. I had a morning flight back home the next day, so I checked the flight time on my ticket, set the alarm on my phone and went to sleep. As soon as the alarm went off, I got up and hurried to the airport. Imagine how surprised I was to find that I'd missed my flight by five hours! I'd misread the time on the ticket. I'd thought it said 8.00 a.m. but in fact, when I put my glasses on, I could see it said 3.00 a.m. I had to wait another eight hours in the airport for the next flight and I had to pay for a new ticket.

✈ 🚉 🚌 **DEPARTURES**

ON TIME
PARIS
LONDON
SYDNEY
NEW YORK
ROME
TOKYO

2

Johnny

I think I've made a huge mistake. I started university in September and I have a horrible feeling that I've chosen the wrong course. I really hate it. I don't understand any of it. I think maybe university was the wrong choice for me. I did quite well in my exams at school, and I thought going to university and living in a flat would be fun. I didn't want to get a job because I think that you get a better job if you've got a degree. Now I feel lonely and stressed and I've lost all my confidence. I'm jealous of my friends who are working instead of being at university. I can't tell my parents because they are so proud that I'm studying. There's nothing I can do though, so I suppose I'll just have to continue.

3

Cosmo

My mistake was really serious. It cost the company I worked for a lot of money, and I lost my job. When it happened, I had been working for my dad's best friend's company for about a year. I was clearing some old files from the computer system when suddenly absolutely everything disappeared. I'd selected all and then pressed *delete*. Because I hadn't realised what I'd done, I pressed *empty trash* too! It was awful. My boss was so upset.

4

Greta

I love animals. We always had lots of pets when I was growing up, and I miss having animals in my life. Two weeks ago, I was walking home when it started to rain heavily and I didn't have an umbrella with me. I ran into the nearest shop, which happened to be a large pet shop. I started looking around while I was waiting for the rain to stop, and I saw the prettiest little white rabbit. It was really cheap and the shop assistant told me that I could easily keep a rabbit in my flat! So I bought the rabbit straight away and brought it home. I really love it, but it's destroying my flat. I've had to replace the cables for my laptop and my lamp because the rabbit ate them, and it has made holes in the carpet. I just don't know what to do!

3 Read the texts again. Are the sentences true (T) or false (F)?

1 Laila's company bought another ticket for her. ......
2 Laila's flight was in the morning. ......
3 Johnny is feeling stressed because of the choice he made. ......
4 Johnny has told his parents about his mistake. ......
5 Greta thinks buying her rabbit was a good idea. ......
6 Greta has a plan to fix her mistake. ......
7 Cosmo was working in his dad's company. ......
8 Cosmo was unable to fix his mistake. ......

4 Choose the correct alternatives.

1 Laila was feeling *ill/ angry* when her mistake happened.
2 Laila had problems *reading/ finding* her ticket.
3 Johnny finds his course *boring/ confusing*.
4 Johnny's parents are *angry with/ pleased with* him.
5 Greta went into the pet shop because *the weather was bad/ her family asked her to.*
6 The rabbit has *damaged things/ injured people* in the flat.
7 Cosmo *removed/ stole* information from his computer.
8 His boss *was/ wasn't* upset about the mistake.

5 Find words in the texts to match the definitions.

1 causing problems for someone, often in a way that is annoying (text 1)
....
2 read something incorrectly (text 1)
....
3 when you feel upset and worried because of things that are happening in your life (text 2)
....
4 when you feel upset because you want something that someone else has got or is doing (text 2)
....
5 when you feel pleased about what you or someone close to you has done (text 2)
....
6 documents or information on a computer (text 3)
....
7 remove text on a computer (text 3)
....
8 causing damage (text 4)
....

6 Read the comment below. Which person in Exercise 2 is Molly replying to?

Hi,

Your post really made me laugh! What a nightmare. What were you thinking? 😄 In the past, I've bought clothes and shoes without thinking, but I've never bought one of those! Well, they say that you learn from your mistakes. I'm sure next time you are about to buy something, you'll stop yourself and think it through more carefully.

Don't worry though – this isn't the biggest mistake in the world. I think you should take it back to the shop and exchange it for a fish.

Maybe you should also choose a new carpet – or buy a rug to cover the holes! 😄 And while you're at the shops, don't forget to buy yourself an umbrella, so that you don't have to shelter in a shop next time it rains!

Good luck!

Molly

7 Read the email again and answer the questions.

1 How does Molly describe the person's situation?
....
2 What has Molly bought without thinking in the past?
....
3 Which animal does Molly suggest the person exchanges it for?
....
4 Which other items does Molly think the person should buy?
....
5 Why should the person buy these items?
....
....
....

Writing

1 Complete the story with the words in the box.

> as   as soon as   but   by the time   despite
> however   then   ~~when~~

I was nearly back at the boat **¹** _when_ I saw it. A large, grey shape gliding softly towards me, cutting through the water like a sharp knife through butter. A strange feeling ran over my body. Panic made me want to swim, but my head told me not to move. I wondered if I could make it back to the boat, **²** _____ the shape was getting closer and closer, larger and larger. I would never make it. I reached for the knife in my belt. **³** _____ , my fingers were shaking and the knife fell into the water below. **⁴** _____ I watched the shape get closer, I realised it was bigger than I'd first imagined. It was enormous! Inside my head I began to say goodbye to the people I loved most. **⁵** _____ suddenly the animal swam into view and I could see that it wasn't a shark but a beautiful whale. **⁶** _____ I realised that this friendly animal would not hurt me, I began laughing and crying at the same time. **⁷** _____ it was near me, I had managed to find my underwater camera. **⁸** _____ the fact that my hands that were still shaking, I took the most amazing photo of it.

2 Read the story again and choose the correct alternatives.

1 The story happened to the *writer/writer's best friend*.
2 *Lots of people experience/Only one person experiences* the event in the story.
3 At first, the writer *couldn't/could* see what kind of animal it was.
4 The writer thought that the animal was a *dolphin/shark*.
5 The writer *dropped/couldn't find* his knife.
6 The writer *attacked/didn't attack* the animal with his knife.
7 The animal *attacked/didn't attack* the writer.
8 The writer *took/didn't take* a photo of the animal.

3 Choose the correct option a, b or c.

1 The burglar ran away _____ he heard the owners return.
   a despite   b as soon as   c however
2 We turned the corner, _____ we heard a terrible noise.
   a however   b despite   c then
3 It was daytime, _____ it was still very dark.
   a but   b then   c by the time
4 The girl was soaking wet _____ she reached the house.
   a despite   b but   c by the time
5 He didn't hear us _____ our shouts and screams.
   a however   b despite   c but
6 The sun was going down _____ the boat sailed away.
   a as   b however   c despite
7 I was about to turn back _____ I saw something on the ground.
   a despite   b when   c as soon as
8 Emma was angry with the boy. _____ , she still felt sorry for him.
   a As   b Then   c However

4 Read the Focus box. Then answer Exercise 5 below.

Creating interest in stories

You can make a short story more interesting by:
- starting or ending with something surprising.
- quickly introducing the location and/or the main characters.
- adding descriptive adjectives and adverbs.
- using similes (phrases that describe something by comparing it to something else).
- describing how people in the story feel.

5 Read the story again. Write words or phrases that show:

1 the location
   in the sea
2 the characters
   _____
3 six descriptive adjectives
   _____
   _____
4 a descriptive adverb
   _____
5 a simile
   _____
6 two sentences describing how the writer is feeling
   _____
   _____

6 Match the sentence halves.

1 The clouds looked like _c_
2 The happy bride was like ___
3 The lake was so still. It was like ___
4 We were so tired that we slept like ___
5 The lonely man was like ___
6 Her clear blue eyes were like ___
7 The snow fell heavily and covered the village like ___
8 The smell in the basement was like ___

a pools of water.
b babies for 12 hours.
c balls of ice cream in the sky.
d a huge white blanket.
e a child at a party.
f vegetables and old shoes.
g a lost dog trying to get home.
h a mirror.

7 Make the story more interesting by adding adjectives or adverbs.

___ was raining ¹ ___ as I approached the ² ___
___ ouse. The door was unlocked so I pushed it ³ ___ .
___ was quiet inside. I called out ⁴ ___ .

__he last time I had been there, it had been full of
___ light and ⁶ ___ noise. This time, however,
__here was just darkness and silence. I felt ⁷ ___ .

___ walked up the ⁸ ___ stairs and headed to the
___ bedroom where I had stayed on my last
__0 ___ visit. It was just as I had left it. The room was
__1 ___ . I sat on the bed and listened to the rain.

Suddenly, I heard footsteps outside. The door of the
bedroom opened ¹² ___ and I couldn't believe who
I saw ...

Prepare

8a **You are going to write a short story. Choose one of the topics from the box.**

| the accident | the mistake | the complaint | the crime |

b Plan your story. Think about the following:

- the characters
  - How many people are in your story?
  - Who is / are the main character(s)?
  - How are they connected to each other?
  - Describe his/her/their personality.
  - Describe his/her/their appearance.
  - Think of some descriptive adjectives or similes you could use.
- the location
  - Where does the story happen?
  - Describe the place. Think of some descriptive adjectives or similes you could use.
  - What time does it happen in? The past, present or future?
- the main action
  - What is the main action?
  - Does it happen at the beginning, middle or end of your story?
- the surprise
  - How can you make your surprise exciting but believable?

c Think of a suitable first line for your story or choose one of the first lines below.

1 I woke up suddenly to the sound of breaking glass.
2 'What have you done?' asked Hannah with a trembling voice.
3 Sadly, Tom turned and walked away.
4 Autumn has always been my favourite season.
5 With his heart pounding, Rahul continued to run as fast as he could.

Write

9 Write your short story. Use your notes from Exercise 8 and the ideas in the Focus box to help you.

5A

Vocabulary

Running a company

1 Choose the correct option a, b or c.

1 We haven't made or lost money this year. We've _____ .
   a broken even   **b** broken down   **c** broken up

2 We're looking to _____ into new markets in Asia and Africa.
   a field   **b** expand   **c** market

3 My _____ are put into my bank account at the end of every month.
   a losses   **b** wages   **c** competitors

4 We're _____ three new products this month.
   a fielding   **b** setting up   **c** launching

5 The business has been in the family for years. It was _____ by my grandfather.
   a broken even   **b** set up   **c** exported

6 We might have to close our business. We've made a _____ for three years in a row.
   a profit   **b** break even   **c** loss

7 Last month, we expanded into new _____ in Mexico and Chile.
   a markets   **b** wages   **c** profits

8 Last year we made a loss, but this year we've made a _____ of €500,000.
   a market   **b** profit   **c** product

2 Complete the text with the correct form of the words in the box.

competitor   expand   export   field   launch   profit
~~take over~~   wages

This has been a great year for us at Parkers International. Since we ¹ _took over_ Harris and Co last September, the company has been doing very well. We've made a healthy ² _____ of $3 million. We've done much better than Mark and Sons, which is our main ³ _____ . We've also performed better than most other companies in our ⁴ _____ . I'd like to thank all our employees. You will be receiving a little extra in your ⁵ _____ this month, as a way to say 'thank you'. Next year, we will continue to ⁶ _____ by growing our business. We're going to ⁷ _____ three new products and we hope to ⁸ _____ them to several countries in Europe.

Grammar

Future forms

3 Read the sentences and tick (✓) the best future form.

1 I predict a profit for the company this year.
   a The company will make a profit this year. ✓
   b The company is making a profit this year.

2 We're going to take over this company.
   a I'm sure we'll take over this company.
   b We probably won't take over this company.

3 We're meeting at 9 a.m. tomorrow.
   a I predict that we'll meet tomorrow at 9 a.m.
   b We've arranged to meet tomorrow at 9 a.m.

4 It's possible that we'll launch a new service next week.
   a We're launching a new service next week.
   b We might launch a new service next week.

5 He's sure that there'll be job losses.
   a There are going to be job losses.
   b There might be job losses.

6 We're going to export products to China next year.
   a They may export products to China next year.
   b They'll export products to China next year.

7 There's a possibility that we'll make a loss this year.
   a We may make a loss this year.
   b We're making a loss this year.

8 We plan to increase wages in September.
   a We'll be increasing wages in September.
   b We won't be increasing wages in September.

4 Choose the option (a, b or c) that <u>can't</u> be used to complete the sentences.

1 I think it _____ today.
   a will rain   **b** rains   **c** is going to rain

2 We _____ the train at 9 a.m. tomorrow morning.
   a caught   **b** are catching   **c** are going to catch

3 He _____ to university in Paris next September.
   a is going   **b** going to go   **c** is going to go

4 It's possible that Harris will win the race. He _____ first.
   a coming   **b** may come   **c** might come

5 This time next week, we _____ on the beach.
   a will be sitting   **b** will be   **c** are sitting

6 Sara has just announced that she _____ married!
   a is getting   **b** is going to get   **c** gets

7 Don't call me at 4 p.m. because I _____ home from work.
   a drive   **b** will be driving   **c** may be driving

8 Frank _____ out with us tonight because he's not very well.
   a isn't going to come   **b** doesn't come
   c isn't coming

9 In five years' time, I _____ 30 years old.
   a 'll be   **b** 'll be being   **c** 'm going to be

Grammar

Adverbs used with the present perfect

1 Put the words in the correct order to make sentences.

1 research / I / finished / yet / haven't / my
I haven't finished my research yet.

2 job / She's / started / new / a / just

3 different / sister / so far / My / had / jobs / has / five

4 thrown away / even / Sue / TV / has / her

5 visited / different / already / We've / capital cities / three

6 been / countries / Europe / We've / only / to / in / two

7 where / next year / We / haven't / still / decided / to go

8 already / students / the party / The / have / left

2 Choose the correct option a, b or c.

1 My boss called me ten minutes ago. I've
_____ been offered a job in Lisbon!

a just   b even   c already

2 They only arrived in Morocco this morning, but they've _____ bought lots of souvenirs.

a so far   b already   c even

3 I've been working at Parsons for six years and I haven't been promoted _____ .

a even   b yet   c already

4 He hasn't heard of any football teams. He hasn't _____ heard of Manchester United!

a even   b yet   c so far

5 I don't watch TV very often. I've _____ watched one programme this month.

a yet   b only   c even

6 _____ , I've eaten three sandwiches, four cakes and a biscuit.

a Even   b Still   c So far

7 I _____ have some cake left over from my birthday.

a already   b still   c just

Vocabulary

New projects

3 Complete the text with the verbs in the box.

> change my mind   got rid of   graduating   offered   quit   sorted out
> ~~struggling~~   went ahead

A few years ago, I was really **1** ___*struggling*___ with the pressure at work. So I decided to **2** _____ my job. My boss tried to **3** _____ about leaving and he even **4** _____ me a pay rise. But I **5** _____ with my plan anyway. I decorated my flat and **6** _____ a lot of possessions. Then I rented my flat to some friends and decided to go travelling. I sat down with my laptop and I **7** _____ an amazing trip of a lifetime! I visited 14 countries in three months! When I came back, I went back to college to study Design Technology. Next week, I'm **8** _____ from university and start my new career!

4 Choose the correct alternatives.

1 Where did you go on your *date/ceremony* last night? Are you going to see him again?

2 We were late for the wedding and missed the whole *ceremony/date*.

3 Have you got *permission/destination* from the council to do the building works?

4 We've sorted out a date for our holiday, but haven't decided on a *permission/destination* yet. We can't make up our minds where to go!

5 My holiday request has been *agreed/allowed* by my boss, so now we can book our trip.

6 I did some work experience at the company but it came to *something/nothing* because I didn't get a job.

5 Match the words in the box with definitions 1–8.

> ceremony   date   destination   graduate   possession   sort out
> struggle

1 organise _____
2 finish a course at university or college _____
3 try hard with something difficult _____
4 a plan to meet a girlfriend or a boyfriend _____
5 a formal event to celebrate or remember something _____
6 a thing that you own _____
7 the place you're going to _____

Vocabulary

Education

1 Write the words and phrases in the box in the correct column in the table below.

> be put off something encourage someone
> give individual attention maintain discipline
> perform badly put pressure on someone
> raise standards ~~succeed~~

positive	negative
succeed	

2 Choose the correct option (a, b or c) to replace the words in bold without changing the meaning.

1 In smaller classes, for example with ten or fewer students, teachers can **teach** more content.
   a encourage b maintain c cover

2 Isaac isn't **achieving** very well in English.
   a exploring b performing c raising

3 In our school we used to **tell the teacher what we thought about** each lesson.
   a give the teacher feedback on
   b raise the teachers' standards on
   c give the teacher individual attention on

4 My year six teacher was terrible because he could never **control the class**.
   a succeed b raise standards
   c maintain discipline

5 I was always **given opportunities** to ask questions at school.
   a encouraged b pressured c performed

6 I felt **that people expected too much of me** when I was doing my exams.
   a the benefit b under pressure c put off

7 My parents always **encouraged me and my sister to** have a go at everything.
   a told us not to b told us to
   c told us it wasn't important

8 Going to university really **isn't the right decision for** everybody.
   a doesn't put off b doesn't encourage
   c doesn't suit

Grammar

Comment adverbs

3 Match the sentence halves.
1 Hopefully, I'll _____
2 Unfortunately, my favourite teacher _____
3 Apparently boys _____
4 Basically, you can't _____
5 Personally, I think _____
6 Generally, people _____
7 Obviously, we haven't _____
8 Actually, I left school _____

a at 16, not 17.
b got time to finish this now.
c do worse than girls at exams, I've heard.
d young people need to learn practical skills.
e learn if you are stressed.
f isn't here this term.
g have good memories of their school years.
h pass my exams.

4 Tick (✓) the sentences with the correct adverb.
1 Hopefully, I'll make it to the party tonight. ✓
2 Luckily, I had revised the right things for the exam.
3 Personally, 80% of people in my year failed at least one exam.
4 James wanted to go to Sussex University, but fortunately, he wasn't accepted.
5 Apparently, many university courses in Iceland are taught in English.
6 Basically, you have to pass your exams if you want to go to university.
7 Hopefully, girls do better than boys in UK schools.
8 Actually, Oxford University is the oldest university in the UK.

Functional language

Agree and disagree

1 Choose the correct alternatives.

A: It really annoys me how much some of these star footballers get paid.

B: I'm afraid **¹**/*kind of agree*/<u>*I don't see it like that*</u>. I think they deserve the money they get.

A: What? That's crazy. They get paid more money in a week than most people get in a lifetime.

B: **²**/*I'm not so sure that's true*/*I half agree*.

A: It is for some of them.

B: **³**/*I don't see it like that*/*I guess*. But they are really talented and they do work really hard.

A: Absolutely! But I'm a really good graphic design artist and I work really hard at my job, but I still don't get paid that kind of money.

B: **⁴**/*I suppose so*/*I'm not so sure that's true*, but they also make lots of money for other people, you know, like their football club, the town they live in, sponsorship, advertising …

A: **⁵**/*I kind of agree*/*It's partly to do with that*, but I think they could be paid half the amount and they'd still be millionaires.

B: **⁶**/*Up to a point*/*Fair point*, but I still think talent deserves rewards.

2 Choose the correct option for the function in brackets.

1 I think eating meat is really bad for you and for the planet.
   (agree but not completely)
   a That's true.   **b** Up to a point.   **c** Absolutely!

2 University education is a complete waste of time. (disagree politely)
   a That's partly true.   **b** I know what you mean.
   c I'm afraid I don't see it like that.

3 I think we have a really strong government at the moment.
   (agree but not completely)
   a I kind of agree.   **b** I'm not so sure that's true.
   c I'm afraid I don't see it like that.

4 Mobile phones are the most amazing inventions ever!
   (agree completely)
   a Absolutely!   **b** Up to a point.   **c** I half agree.

5 The world would be a better place if everyone smiled at each other in the street. (agree completely)
   a You might be right.   **b** I guess so.   **c** Sure.

6 It's not worth going on holiday in the summer – everywhere's too busy.
   (agree reluctantly)
   a I suppose so.   **b** Fair point.   **c** That's true.

Listening

1 🔊 **5.01 Listen to the radio interview. Who is Anna Marchant?**
Anna Marchant is a …
   a chef
   b radio presenter
   c restaurant owner

2 Listen again. Are the sentences true (T) or false (F)?

1 Anna's new project is to open a café.
   F

2 She developed the idea for the new place with her husband. ....

3 It's going to be in the centre of the new town. ....

4 She's going to call it *Green Leaves*. ....

5 'Foraging' means finding and collecting food. ....

6 Anna won't need to buy any food. ....

7 There was a problem with the floor of the building. ....

8 The opening party is in July. ....

3 Listen again, and guess the meaning of the words and phrases in italics.

1 … the program that *keeps you up to date* …
   a informs you
   b tells you when

2 *I'm in the process of* …
   a I've started but not finished
   b I've recently finished

3 *Fabulous.*
   a strange
   b great

4 … local, *seasonal* food.
   a available in every season
   b available only at certain times of year

5 … won't be able to forage for everything on the menu, *presumably*?
   a I guess
   b fortunately

6 … now we're having a *launch party*
   a party to celebrate the beginning of something
   b party to celebrate the end of something

Reading

1 **Read the article and choose the best title.**

   a Modern Problems for Young People

   b Happiness Begins at Home

   c Children of the Future

2 **Read the article and put topics 1–5 in the order they appear.**

   a Travelling   ....

   b Eating dinner as a family   ....

   c Limiting the use of technology   ....

   d Changes in society   _1_

   e Doing jobs at home   ....

A People often focus on education as a way to help children grow into successful adults. However, it is worth considering the importance of parents and home life in this process. According to research, what happens at home may actually have a larger influence on us than what happens at school.

B Our society has changed a lot in the last 30 or 40 years. The organisation of many families has changed. These days there are many single parent families and families where both parents go out to work. It is also true that many grandparents are less involved than they used to be in the past. Our social life has changed as technology has advanced. We now live much of our lives on mobile devices. Many children communicate with other children through online game playing, social media sites and messaging. We also have 24/7 access to entertainment. This has all had a big effect on our children.

C So, what do researchers believe is the way to promote well-being and success for our children? Firstly, they say that children benefit from eating dinner with their families at least five times a week. It encourages a sense of being part of a group and provides a space to talk.

D It's also important to limit the amount of time a child spends using tablets and smartphones. Apparently, too much time spent on these devices can lead to a lack of focus, attention, vocabulary and social skills. Instead, parents are advised to read to their younger children and to encourage older children to read for themselves.

E Research also shows that giving children chores to do around the home can help them become successful adults who can focus on a task and understand that a job needs to be done. Although children do well when their parents are with them as much as possible, apparently there can be benefits for girls who have working mothers. It seems that seeing their mothers have careers, encourages young women to do well both academically and at work.

F Finally, researchers say you should take your children on holiday. Research shows that people who travel more as children, especially when they go abroad, grow up into positive and successful adults. Travel encourages children to explore, be open-minded and to learn from their experiences.

3 Read the article again and choose the best heading for paragraphs A–F. There are two headings you do not need.

1 Becoming successful adults   *A*
2 Seeing the world   ....
3 Eating together   ....
4 Taking time out   ....
5 Why do we need to think about this?   ....
6 Turn it off and read   ....
7 The need for individual attention   ....
8 Positive attitudes to work   ....

4 Read the article again and answer the questions.

According to the article …

1 What has changed a lot in the last 30 to 40 years?

2 Why have our social lives changed?

3 What activity provides children with a space to talk?

4 Which activity can negatively affect children's ability to focus in school?

5 What helps children understand that jobs need to be done?

6 Who benefits from having a mother who works?

7 What activity encourages children to explore?

8 Where is it best to travel with children?

5 Find words in the article to match definitions 1–8.

1 a series of actions that have a particular result (paragraph A)
   process
2 have an effect on what happens (paragraph A)

3 be able to use something (paragraph B)

4 the feeling of being healthy and happy (paragraph C)

5 restrict (paragraph D)

6 an absence (paragraph D)

7 jobs that you do around the home (paragraph E)

8 able to accept other people's ideas and opinions (paragraph F)

6 Read the magazine interview. Which of the activities from the article is mentioned?

Interviewer: Georgina Hayley, you are, probably, the most successful businesswoman in the world today. So, what is the secret of your success?

Georgina: Well, I suppose luck is a big part of it. I have a very supportive family and I was lucky to have a great education. My parents made a lot of sacrifices so I could go to university.

Interviewer: That's true. However, that's also true of a lot of other people who haven't become as successful as you.

Georgina: I suppose it is, yes.

Interviewer: So would you say that you are just naturally clever?

Georgina: No, in fact I struggled at school. But I had some great teachers who encouraged me and my parents always taught me that it's OK to fail. When you fail, you ask yourself why you failed and then you just start again and do it differently the next time.

Interviewer: So you never give up?

Georgina: No. They taught me that you have to keep trying and that you have to work hard. My parents also gave me jobs to do around the house as a child.

Interviewer: So, do you think it's important for children to do chores?

Georgina: Yes, it's very important. They have to learn life skills. Having chores taught me to be responsible and value hard work.

Interviewer: But if children are really busy, will they have time to play or meet friends? Free time is important, too, isn't it?

Georgina: Absolutely! Children need to be able to have fun, relax and see friends. It's about finding the right balance.

7 Choose the correct alternatives.

1 Georgina Hayley is a *teacher / businesswoman*.
2 She had a *bad / good* education.
3 She *performed well / didn't perform well* at school.
4 She thinks her parents *put pressure on / didn't put pressure on* her to be successful all the time.
5 She believes failure can be a *positive / negative* thing.
6 When she was a child, her parents gave her lots of *chores to do / free time* at home.
7 She *thinks / doesn't think* that she is very responsible.
8 Georgina thinks that socialising *is also / isn't* important for children.

Writing

1 **Read the introduction to the essay. What is the topic?**
   a Public transport
   b Working from home
   c Office politics

2 **Complete the essay with the words and phrases in the box.**

> as well as   for example   however   I believe
> in short   while

3 **Which statement best describes the writer's opinion?**
   a The writer is against home working.
   b The writer thinks that there will be more home working in the future.
   c The writer is worried about the negative effects of home working.

4 **Match paragraphs A–D to functions 1–4:**
   1 Introduce your first main point. ....
   2 State what the topic is and what the main dilemma of the topic is. Include an overall view of your opinion. ....
   3 Summarise and repeat your overall opinion. ....
   4 Introduce your second main point. ....

5 **Read the Focus box then match supporting examples 1–3 below with paragraphs B–D in the essay.**

Using supporting examples

When writing an essay, it is usual to support opinions with examples. These examples may be from your general knowledge and can include stories in the news, reports, statistics or quotes from experts. You can introduce these supporting examples with the phrase *for example*, but often you don't use a linking word or phrase.
Home working can make employees more stressed. For example, imagine there's a document you need in order to get on with your work. You send an email to a colleague, but you don't receive an answer immediately. You sit there, waiting and waiting for a reply. This can be very frustrating.

   1 A recent study found that most office workers spend a minimum of two hours a day talking to their colleagues. ....
   2 Imagine when you want a second opinion on something, but you have no one to ask. ....
   3 For example, one large technology company organises social events for employees that work at home more than three days a week. ....

Is working from home the perfect way to deal with office politics and crowded public transport? Will it make us happier, healthier people or is it actually creating lonely employees?

A For many modern workers, their journey to work is less than a minute, and their office clothes generally include pyjamas and slippers. This is because working from home is on the increase. Some people believe this is the perfect working arrangement. It means that you can pop out to the shops in the middle of the day, have that tenth cup of coffee without anyone raising eyebrows, and, most importantly for many, no boss watching what you are doing. **1** _____, I would like to argue that this is not the whole story, as working from home can also negatively affect workers.

B **2** _____ it keeps costs down for companies and travel time down for employees, home working also leaves people feeling alone and without support. They sit on their own in a room or space in their house and may not talk to or see anyone for the whole day. This cannot be good for someone's mental or social well-being. Humans are sociable animals, which means that we need to be around other humans.

C **3** _____ cutting people off from social contact, home working can make employees feel more stressed. **4** _____, imagine there's a document you need in order to get on with your work. You send an email to a colleague, but you don't receive an answer immediately. You sit there, waiting and waiting for a reply. This can be very frustrating.

D **5** _____, we need to be aware of the negative effect that home working can have on some people. **6** _____ that companies should make sure their employees have regular contact with each other and with their bosses, have the opportunity to socialise with colleagues and get the support they need.

6 Read another essay on the same topic. Why does this writer disagree with the first writer?

> **Why working from home helps achieve a healthy work-life balance.**
>
> More and more people today are working from home. Some people work from home all the time, while others work from home just a few days a week. **1** ....
>
> It is true that homeworkers sometimes feel isolated from the people and events in the office. However, I would argue that the benefits of working from home far outweigh any disadvantages.
>
> It is clear that working from home is more cost effective for the employer and the employee. **2** ....
>
> As well as being cost effective, homeworkers say that they are more productive at home than they would be in an office. They get more work done in less time. **3** ....
>
> What's more, working from home helps employees to achieve a better work-life balance. The flexibility allows them to work around their friends and family. **4** ....
>
> In short, I believe that homeworking is the future. **5** .... It's time to let go of traditional ideas about business and embrace the future.

7 Complete the essay with the supporting examples a–f. There is one example you do not need.

  a My colleagues who work from home tell me that they aren't distracted by office noise or interrupted by colleagues.

  b A recent report shows that most of the population prefer to work in a place with other people.

  c In a recent talk, business leader Geoffery Marsh said that he believes that 90% of his employees will be working from home by the year 2025.

  d In fact, a recent report has found that 70% of people around the world work from home at least once a week.

  e Reports have found that homeworkers are happier, healthier and less stressed than office workers.

  f For example, the employer doesn't need to provide a desk space, equipment or insurance for a homeworker. Meanwhile, the employee doesn't need to pay any travel expenses.

8 Look at the examples of *however* and *while* in the essay on page 42 and match the sentence halves.

  1 We use *however* ....
  2 We use *while* ....

  a either at the beginning or in the middle of two clauses to show that there is a contrast between them.

  b when you are adding a new sentence or comment that contains information that contrasts with what came before. If it begins a sentence, it is followed by a comma.

9 Choose the correct alternatives.

  1 *However/While* it's important that we protect the rainforests, we must also look after the people who are living there.

  2 I believe that social media can be harmful to young brains. *However/While*, a recent report has suggested that it can help them to develop.

  3 Robots may be able to take the place of employees in some roles. *However/While*, they will never be able to provide that human touch.

  4 More and more people are now working from home. *However/While* this means that there are fewer people using public transport, we must continue to invest in the system.

  5 *However/While* technology means that we can do our work more quickly, it doesn't necessarily mean that we have more free time.

Prepare

10a Choose one of these topics for your essay.

  1 There should be more older people in the workplace, as they can offer lots of useful experience.

  2 Although having qualifications can provide people with job opportunities, this also means that they don't want to do unskilled work.

  b Plan your essay. Make notes about:
  - your opinion
  - two main points to support your opinion
  - an example to support each main point
  - a closing statement that summarises and repeats your opinion on the topic

Write

11 Write your essay. Use your notes in Exercise 10 and the information in the Focus box to help you.

6A

Vocabulary
At the cinema, on TV

1 Choose the correct alternatives.

I love watching TV! I'm a big fan **1**_of_/on soap operas. One minute, they're making **2**_me_/my laugh at some hilarious scene and the next minute I'm **3**on/in tears because they're killing **4**on/off my favourite character!
I really don't like talent shows, though. Watching somebody get voted **5**on/off each week isn't my idea of fun. It's enough to get me to switch **6**over/on.

2 Match definitions 1–8 with the words in the box.

blockbuster   dialogue   ending   episode   filming
~~scene~~   series   special effects

1 a single part of action that happens in one place
scene
2 a set of episodes ....
3 parts of a TV series/film created by computer
....
4 the final part of a TV series/film ....
5 a conversation in a TV series/film ....
6 one part of a TV series ....
7 the process of recording the action onto film
....
8 a film that makes a lot of money ....

3 Replace the words in bold in the sentences with words in the box so that the meaning stays the same.

characters   dull   hilarious   is a fan of   ~~tense~~
useless

1 I felt **worried** when I watched the characters have a fight.
tense
2 This TV programme is **so funny**! ....
3 I think that cookery programmes are **boring**. ....
4 The singer was **very bad** and got voted off in the first week. ....
5 He **really likes** the new drama series. ....
6 The **people in the TV series** are awful! ....

Grammar
Passive

4 Put the words in the correct order to make sentences.

1 at / shown / The / Wednesday / 8 p.m. / is / series / every
The series is shown every Wednesday at 8 p.m.
2 done / the studio / The / were / special effects / in
....
3 Famous / this / get made / TV programmes / in / studio
....
4 are being / more / used to be / Actors / paid / than / they
....
5 had been / one / was cancelled / Only / episode / made / before / the series
....
6 cut / This / the episode / scene / is going / from / to be
....
7 filmed / Europe / The / series / new / will / in / be
....
8 has been / weeks / This / two / in / produced / episode
....

5 Rewrite the sentences in the passive form.

1 People make many new TV programmes every year.
Many new TV programmes are made every year.
2 People had offered the actor lots of parts before this one.
....
3 Someone produced this TV programme very well.
....
4 People pay some actors millions of dollars for every film.
....
5 Someone is going to kill off that character in the next episode.
....
6 Someone has cut up this episode into short scenes.
....
7 People are filming that scene at the moment.
....
8 Millions of people will use the new streaming service next year.
....

Vocabulary

Services and recommendations

1 Complete the sentences with the words in the box.

> assessed   deliver   did   fixed   look at   made
> removed   ~~replace~~

1 Frances had to ___replace___ the windscreen on her car after the accident.
2 Paul used his motorbike to _____ the pizzas to people's homes.
3 The builder _____ the condition of the roof after the storm.
4 Raoul _____ the television so it's working again now.
5 Zara _____ her make up before she went out for the evening.
6 The students _____ the graffiti from the wall before their teacher saw it.
7 We need to _____ the situation and think about how we can improve it.
8 My daughter _____ a cake for my birthday.

2 Choose the correct alternatives.

The builders Cole and Sons installed our new kitchen last week. They did the work while we were on holiday, which was very **1**_convenient/conversation_ for us. I would give Cole and Sons four stars **2**_out of/up to_ five for service. They arrived **3**_on/of_ time and they cleared up the **4**_message/mess_ they made. Also, they were **5**_efficient/official_ because they got the job done in the time they said they would. They did a better job than another builder I got to do work on my house last year. He was **6**_useful/useless_ and did a terrible job. Never again!

It's important to have people working in your home who you can **7**_trust/treat_. I would rather have someone who is **8**_renewable/reliable_ than someone who is cheap. Actually, the price that Cole and Sons charged us for our kitchen was quite **9**_reason/reasonable_!

Grammar

have/get something done

3 Match the sentence halves.

1 She's having her hair ___h___
2 You can get your mobile phone screen _____
3 He's had repairs _____
4 She has to get the hole in the roof _____
5 Samira got her fitness _____
6 Thomas had his car window _____
7 My aunt has her nails _____
8 You can have your car _____

a replaced at this shop.
b done to his house.
c assessed at the gym.
d done once a month.
e fixed before it rains again.
f washed at the garage.
g broken while he was on holiday.
h cut at the hairdresser's.

4 Complete the sentences using the noun and verb in brackets and the correct form of _have/get something done._

1 Sarah ___gets her nails done___ (her nails/do) every two weeks.
2 I _____ (my car/fix) at the moment.
3 Last week, Tim _____ (a tooth/remove) at the dentist.
4 Stephen _____ (nose/break) in a fight yesterday.
5 She _____ (passport/take away) at the airport last week.
6 He can _____ (his tyre/replace) at the new garage.
7 I _____ (hair/do) at this salon for four years.

5 Find and correct five mistakes in sentences 1–8.

1 I had my toenails /~~did~~ last week.
    done

2 They got an album made of their wedding photos.

3 You can get your broken light fixed at the garage.

4 We had some Chinese food delivering an hour ago.

5 Did you get your tooth looked at yesterday?

6 He made his wallet stolen yesterday.

7 We're having our house paint at the moment.

8 Diane gets cleaned her car every month.

Vocabulary

In the news

1 Match the sentence halves.

1 Their goalkeeper has been hit by _c_
2 Workers have gone ....
3 The man has been found ....
4 Supermarkets are trying to get ....
5 The judge told the boy to keep ....
6 People have carried out several opinion ....
7 There are fears that Chelsea's star ....
8 New drugs for the treatment ....

a rid of leftover food.
b polls about the election.
c injury and won't play in tomorrow's final.
d of the illness will be available next year.
e player has been injured.
f out of trouble or he would end up in prison.
g on strike because of low pay.
h guilty of theft.

2 Match definitions 1–8 with the words in the box.

breakthrough   opinion poll   profits   quit   scandal
sentence   strike   ~~union~~

1 a group of workers that tries to improve working
   conditions   _union_
2 to leave a job   ....
3 an important discovery after a lot of work has
   been done   ....
4 a survey of people's ideas   ....
5 a shocking event   ....
6 money you make when you sell something for more
   than you paid for it   ....
7 a punishment from a law court   ....
8 a period of time when workers stop working
   ....

Grammar

Probability

3 Choose the correct alternatives.

1 **A:** Do you think that the two sides will sign the
       agreement?
   B: Yes, I do and _there's a good chance it will_/
       it probably won't happen today.
2 **A:** Do you think this decision will help workers?
   B: Yes, absolutely. _It's bound to_/ _It probably won't_ help
       all of us.
3 **A:** Do you think this drug will slow the development of
       the disease?
   B: I'm not sure. It _definitely won't_/ _might_ slow it down
       a bit.
4 **A:** Do you think your party will win the election?
   B: No, they _are bound to_/ _definitely won't_ win.
5 **A:** Do you think this opinion poll is correct?
   B: Well, you can never be sure. But _it's fairly likely that it will_/
       it definitely won't be close to the final result.
6 **A:** Do you think the manager will sell your star player?
   B: No way! _He's bound to._/ _He definitely won't._
7 **A:** Do you think the leader will quit after the election?
   B: Maybe. _He'll definitely_/ _He might_ want to do
       something else.
8 **A:** Do you think it'll be hot today?
   B: Yes, look at that blue sky. _It'll definitely_/
       It probably won't be sunny!

4 Read the sentences and tick the correct meaning.

1 There's a good chance that the president will visit.
   a The president will probably visit. ✓
   b The president probably won't visit.
2 This scandal is bound to damage the company.
   a This scandal will almost certainly damage the company.
   b This scandal almost certainly won't damage the
       company.
3 I doubt the team's star player is going to score today.
   a The team's star player is probably going to score today.
   b The team's star player probably isn't going to score
       today.
4 There's a small chance that there will be a storm tomorrow.
   a There will almost certainly be a storm tomorrow.
   b There probably won't be a storm tomorrow.
5 It's unlikely that the unions will reach an agreement today.
   a The unions will probably reach an agreement today.
   b The unions probably won't reach an agreement today.
6 Workers will definitely go on strike tomorrow.
   a Workers are bound to go on strike tomorrow.
   b Workers are unlikely to go on strike tomorrow.
7 It's fairly likely that profits will be higher than last year.
   a Profits will probably be higher than last year.
   b Profits almost certainly won't be higher than last year.
8 I doubt the boss will quit today.
   a The boss will almost certainly quit today.
   b The boss almost certainly won't quit today.

Functional language
Apologise and make excuses

1 Complete the conversation with the words in the box.

> afraid   impossible   least   make   ~~really~~
> understanding   worry   would

A: I'm [1] _____really_____ sorry, but I'm
[2] _____ I can't meet for dinner tonight.

B: Oh, that's a shame.

A: I [3] _____ if I could, but I'm afraid it's
[4] _____ . I have to go and see my
grandmother. She's gone into hospital.

B: I'm sorry to hear that.

A: I'll [5] _____ it up to you.

B: At [6] _____ you phoned and you didn't leave
me sitting in the restaurant by myself!

A: Thanks for being so [7] _____ !

B: Don't [8] _____ about it. I hope your
grandmother is OK.

2 Put the words in the correct order to complete the
conversation.

A: [1] I can't come / but / sorry, / I'm / the project meeting /
tomorrow / terribly / to
I'm terribly sorry, but I can't come to the project
meeting tomorrow.

B: Oh, dear. Why not?

A: I have to go and see a client. [2] can't / Honestly, / it / get /
I / out / really / of

_____

_____

B: Couldn't you change your client meeting?

A: [3] nothing / really / I / about / do / There's / can / point /
it / at / this

_____

_____

B: Oh well. [4] things / happen / These

_____

A: [5] assure / again / me / you / Let / won't / it / that /
happen

_____

_____

B: [6] what / It / is / is / it

_____

A: [7] only / apologise / I / can

_____

B: Don't worry about it. I'll send you minutes of the
meeting, so you know what you need to do on the
Hamptons project.

A: [8] make / I'll / priority / it / a

_____

Listening

1 🔊 6.01 **Listen to the conversation. What are Nina
and Hassan talking about?**

a how to win talent shows

b what makes a good movie

c TV programmes and films they've enjoyed recently

2 Listen again and complete the sentences with the
words in the box.

> Australia   Derek Sams   Los Angeles   Martin Harris
> _The Day of Arrival_   _The Sound Garden_
> ~~_This Beautiful World_~~   _True or Terrible_

1 Nina has just finished watching a series called
This Beautiful World .

2 In the final scene of this series, they killed off the main
character, _____

3 Hassan is enjoying a talent show called
_____ .

4 The talent show is made in _____ .

5 Hassan saw a film about two brothers. It was called
_____ .

6 The film about the brothers is set in
_____ .

7 One of the brothers is played by _____ .

8 Hassan also saw a science fiction film called
_____ .

3 Listen again. Are these statements true (T) or false (F)?

1 Nina felt happy when she watched the ending of the
series she has just finished.   _F_

2 The ending of the series was well acted.   ____

3 Last night, a comedian was voted off the talent show
that Hassan likes watching.   ____

4 Nina likes TV programmes with a good script and
realistic characters.   ____

5 The brothers in the film that Hassan watched work in a
restaurant.   ____

6 Hassan thinks that Nina should see the science fiction
film at the cinema.   ____

7 Nina doesn't go to the cinema very often because it
costs too much money.   ____

8 Nina likes watching films in bed.   ____

Reading

1 Look at the articles. Which of them features positive news?

2 Read the articles again. Match the sub-headings to the articles.

1. Weather office warns about floods in the south   _C_
2. Tom Peterson hears his sentence today   ____
3. Northover & Co may be hiding profits   ____
4. Large bank announces profits up by 8%   ____
5. Gene discovery may improve treatment   ____

A   BREAKTHROUGH IN CANCER TREATMENT

Scientists have made a breakthrough in cancer treatment because they now understand the genes connected to some cancers. There's a good chance that this will help doctors provide better treatment to cancer patients. Dr Simon Burrows told this paper that traditional forms of treatment could change because doctors will be able to identify which patients are most likely to benefit from new drugs.

B   SCANDAL HITS MAJOR TV COMPANY

Several former employees have claimed that Northover & Co wasn't honest when it published its financial results. They said that the company has hidden millions of dollars in bank accounts overseas. It's likely that work on Northover & Co TV programmes will have to stop while police look at its accounts. We asked company managers to comment on these reports, but nobody was available to speak to our journalists.

C   RECORD RAINFALL BRINGS POSSIBILITY OF FLOODS

Thunderstorms will continue today and it is possible that some rivers will flood. The water level in the River Rowe is dangerously high. The weather office has warned that there is a chance of damage to public transport systems and some roads may also be flooded. Passengers are advised to check transport websites for more information before they travel. The rain will probably last until Sunday evening, but there may be more rain to come later in the week.

D   Football star guilty of dangerous driving

Tom Peterson, star player for Chesterham United, was arrested for dangerous driving after hitting a pedestrian with his car. 'He was going too fast', said Teresa Raymond's of Chesterham. 'He tried to slow down when he saw me crossing the road, but he still hit me. I'm lucky – if he hadn't slowed down, I would have been killed.'

E   New Market Ltd rise in profits

New Market Ltd, one of the largest banks in the country, has announced that its profits have increased by 8 percent since last year. This follows a difficult few years for the bank when they had to make some hard decisions. They closed several local banks and hundreds of employees lost their jobs. The CEO of the bank, Morgan Peters, said, 'We're very pleased with this year's results and there's a good chance that we'll see more rises next year.'

3 Match articles A–E with speakers 1–5.

1

> I was going to drive to see Mum on Sunday, but I think I'll postpone my trip because I don't like driving in the rain.

_C_

2

> I can't believe it! I love watching some of this company's TV programmes! I hope they don't end up cancelling their shows.

....

3

> I lost my job at that bank two years ago. I'm glad to see they're making money again now. Some of us aren't as lucky though. I'm still looking for a job that pays as much as that one did.

....

4

> Just because people are famous, they think they can do anything they like. They should send him to prison to teach him a lesson.

....

5

> This is very good news. I wonder if my grandfather might benefit from these new drugs.

....

4 Answer the questions.

Article A

1 What discovery has been made into cancer research?
  Scientists now understand the genes of some cancers.

2 How can this discovery help patients?
  ....

Article B

3 Who has said that Northover & Co may have broken the law?
  ....

4 Where might the company have hidden money?
  ....

Article C

5 What advice have travellers been given?
  ....

6 How long is the rain going to continue?
  ....

Article D

7 Why was Tom Peterson driving dangerously?
  ....

8 How was Teresa Raymond lucky?
  ....

Article E

9 How much have profits at New Market Ltd risen by since last year?
  ....

10 What difficult decisions has the bank made over the last few years?
  ....

5 Complete the sentences with the proper nouns from the articles.

1 _Dr Simon Burrows_ is the scientist who has made an important discovery in cancer research.

2 _____ is the TV company that might have been hiding some money.

3 _____ is the name of the person who is in charge of the bank.

4 _____ is the football player who drove dangerously.

5 _____ is the name of the football player's team.

6 _____ is the name of the person who was hit by the football player's car.

7 _____ is the name of the bank that has made more money than last year.

8 The _____ is the river where floods might happen.

6 Find words in the text to match definitions 1–8.

1 say who or what someone or something is _identify_ (article A)

2 get an advantage from something _____ (article A)

3 in another country _____ (article B)

4 a record of the money a company receives and spends _____ (article B)

5 cause to become full of water, often causing problems _____ (article C)

6 a person walking in a public place _____ (article D)

7 money that a company makes by doing business _____ (article E)

8 got bigger _____ (article E)

Writing

1 Read the report. Which of these statements is true according to the report?

a Older people share more selfies than others because they have more holidays.

b 18–25-year-olds share more images than any other age group.

c Getting 'likes' is just as important to both sexes.

A Introduction

This report describes the results of a survey to find out about sharing images online. Last February, the survey was given to 100 people between the ages of 18 and 65. They were asked about how and why they share photographs and videos online.

B Main findings

The survey found differences in the way young and older people share images online. Older people are more likely to share photos of holidays, while it is popular for young people to share selfies. Only 14 percent of people over the age of 35 share photos of themselves once a week or more, whereas the majority of people aged between 18 and 25 do and almost one third of them share selfies every day.

Young people also say it's more important that people like their images. Twice as many 18–25-year-olds say it's important to receive 'likes' and 'shares' than adults aged 25–65. There are also differences between the sexes. Nine percent of women said this was very important compared to only four percent of men.

C Conclusion

The survey results suggest that people of all ages enjoy sharing images online. It appears that young people like to share images to show others how happy they are. More research on the subject needs to be done but it is feared that this need for 'likes' and 'shares' could lead to more problem for young people in the future.

2 Read the Focus box. Then answer the questions about the report below.

Organising information

To write a simple report about a survey, use headings to organise it:

Introduction

- Explain what the survey is about, who conducted it and when
- Use the passive to do this: *the survey was given to 100 people; they were asked about …*

Main findings

- Say what the most important finding is in the first sentence, but don't give reasons for it.
- Give one or two statistics to support this finding. You don't have to quote them all.
- If you have more than one topic in the survey, discuss each one in a different paragraph.
- To describe a contrast, use words like: *while, in contrast, whereas, compared to.*
- To describe statistics, use a variety of language: *14%, the majority, almost one third.*

Conclusions

- Explain what you think the survey results mean. Use phrases such as *the results suggest …* and *it appears that …*
- Sometimes you might want to make a recommendation: *More research is needed on this subject.*

Introduction

1 What is the survey about?

2 When did the survey take place?

3 Who took part in it?

Main findings

4 What is the main finding?

5 Find one example of a statistic. What does it refer to? How is it shown?

6 Find one example of contrasting words. Which things are being contrasted?

Conclusion

7 What are the conclusions?

8 What language is used to introduce the conclusions?

3 Choose the correct alternatives.

1 One hundred people *interviewed/were interviewed* for the survey.
2 They were *asked/asking* about why they post photos online.
3 Younger people like to edit their selfies, *while/when* older people don't usually do this.
4 Almost one *third/three* of people said they feel it is important to them to look good online.
5 It *appears/announces* that this can have a negative effect on some people.
6 The *most/majority* of all young people post selfies online.
7 Fifteen percent of people like to post photos of friends *compare/compared* to twenty percent of people who like to post photos of pets and animals.
8 The results *surprise/suggest* that most young people care about what others think of them.

4 Match the descriptions of the statistics to the correct figures.

1 Nearly all the people we spoke to agreed. ....
2 A large majority of women expect more. ....
3 One out of every five teens we spoke to said yes. ....
4 A tiny percentage of people over 65 disagreed. ....
5 A quarter of people refused to answer. ....
6 Just over half of people want changes. ....
7 Almost two thirds of men chose not to answer. ....
8 Less than half of children have access to it. ....

a 0.5%   b 80%   c 98.5%
d 20%   e 53%   f 65%
g 46%   h 25%

Prepare

5 You're going to write a report about a survey of TV viewing habits. Look at the graphs that show the responses to two questions from the survey. Plan what you're going to include in your report.

* Make a note of what the survey is about, when it was done and who was interviewed.
* Decide on the most important finding.
* Choose one or two statistics to support this finding and/or a contrast you can show.
* Decide about one or two conclusions you could make from this finding about the future or a recommendation you could make.
* Decide on a recommendation you could make for the future.

Question 1

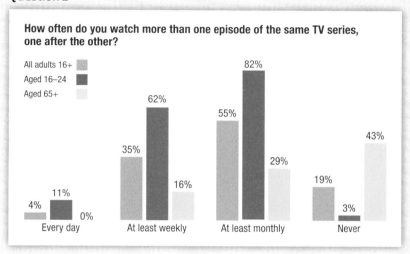

How often do you watch more than one episode of the same TV series, one after the other?

Question 2

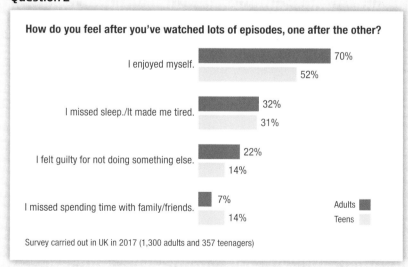

How do you feel after you've watched lots of episodes, one after the other?

Survey carried out in UK in 2017 (1,300 adults and 357 teenagers)

Write

6 Write your report. Use your notes from Exercise 5 and ideas from the Focus box to help you.

Vocabulary

Health problems

1 **Match the sentence halves.**

1   That fish I ate last night really didn't   *f*
2   This cold is making me feel really out   ....
3   John looks exhausted and he's got big bags   ....
4   Luca has gone to see the doctor because he keeps   ....
5   I think I've got an allergic   ....
6   Tom fell off his bike and got a nasty   ....

a   of breath.
b   under his eyes.
c   cut on his nose.
d   reaction to this new face cream.
e   getting a pain in his chest.
f   agree with me.

2 **Match words 1–8 with definitions a–h.**

1   ache   2   allergic   3   cut   4   pale   5   sore
6   strain   7   temperature   8   virus

a   an injury caused by something sharp   ....
b   to injure a muscle in your body   ....
c   something that causes illness   ....
d   a pain that doesn't stop   *1*
e   how hot or cold you are   ....
f   very light in colour   ....
g   unable to eat, touch or smell something because it makes you physically ill   ....
h   painful   ....

3 **Complete the sentences with the missing words.**

1   Lucia had to go to the hospital because she fell and b................ her arm.
2   Please could you get me a glass of water? I've got a really sore t................ .
3   Natasha's leg is really badly b................ . It's all purple.
4   If I eat strawberries, I get an a................ r................ around my mouth.
5   I'm having difficulty bending down because my back is quite s................ .
6   Manon i................ her shoulder playing tennis last week, so she won't be able to play again for a month.

Grammar

Verb patterns 1

4 **Find and correct five mistakes in sentences 1–8.**

1   My dad has pains in his chest, but he's refusing ~~seeing~~ a doctor.   *to see*
2   I keep to get a pain in my knee.
3   I forgot to buy some more cream for my rash at lunchtime.
4   I really hate having a headache.
5   I don't enjoy to go to the doctor's.
6   Lila's just starting to feel better again.
7   I hope being out of hospital by next week.
8   I tried finding some information about the disease on the internet.

5 **Match each pair of sentences with their meanings.**

1   1   Mr Dougal didn't remember to take his medicine yesterday.   *b*
    2   Mr Dougal didn't remember taking his medicine yesterday.   *a*

    a   Mr Dougal did take his medicine, but can't remember doing so.
    b   Mr Dougal didn't take his medicine.

2   1   Try to go to the gym more frequently.   ....
    2   Try going to the gym more frequently.   ....

    a   I realise it may be difficult for you to go to the gym more frequently, but I think you should do it.
    b   I recommend that you go to the gym more frequently.

3   1   Henri stopped smoking five years ago.   ....
    2   Henri stopped to smoke a cigarette.   ....

    a   Henri used to smoke but doesn't anymore.
    b   Henri was doing something, but stopped and had a cigarette.

4   1   I remember reading the instructions.   ....
    2   I remembered to read the instructions.   ....

    a   I read the instructions – I didn't forget!
    b   I read the instructions and I remember that I did it.

Grammar
Verb patterns 2

1 Put the words in the correct order to make sentences.

1 they'll / I / buy / new / a / car / bet

2 for / married / Do / think / money / him / his / you / Elisa?

3 if / Matt / I / earns / than / wonder / more / me

4 Poppy / would / buy / said / dinner / she / tonight

5 rent / I / finding / difficult / that / pay / imagine / he's / to / his / it

6 say / Did / you'd / you / saved / nearly / money / enough?

7 afford / We / couldn't / the / new / realised / flat / we

8 buy / another / I / don't / should / pair / shoes / I / think / of

9 know / meeting / where / we're / Lisa / Do / you?

10 Chris / when / pay increase / know / he'll / doesn't / get / a

2 Complete the sentences with one word in each gap.

1 I think _____that_____ we should save some money this month.
2 I don't know _____ I can afford to go on holiday.
3 I wonder _____ the new sofa will arrive. I hope it's here before the weekend.
4 _____ you realise we've been working here for five years now?
5 I imagine _____ the new boss will bring some new people into the company.
6 _____ you know what the salary is for the manager's job?
7 I don't understand _____ she gets her money from.
8 I'm sure _____ Elena likes her job very much.

3 Choose the correct option a, b or c.

1 He _____ he doesn't know where the money came from.
   a thinks   b claims   c realises
2 I _____ that he's quite rich.
   a ask   b tell   c imagine
3 I _____ I could make more money if I set up my own business, so I left my job.
   a told   b decided   c claimed
4 I don't _____ what Kate's job title is.
   a know   b think   c bet
5 I _____ that money isn't everything.
   a agree   b claim   c wonder
6 Did you _____ Jeremy what time to meet us?
   a know   b remember   c tell
7 I _____ if they can really afford their new house.
   a wonder   b imagine   c suppose
8 I _____ that I owe Paula £20.
   a asked   b told   c forgot

Vocabulary
Money

4 Complete the text with the correct form of the verbs in the box.

| afford | ~~buy~~ | earn | lend | owe | pay |
| take | win | | | | |

My husband and I have been trying to
1 _to buy_ a bigger house for about two years. We both have jobs, and we are both
2 _____ quite good salaries. However, the town we live in has become very popular and we just can't 3 _____ anything here anymore. We've asked the bank 4 _____ us the money, but they won't increase our mortgage. Even if they did, it would
5 _____ all our earnings each month to pay back the loan. I can't ask my parents for any money because they 6 _____ for some building work on our house last year, and we still 7 _____ them the money for that. We've decided the only way to get the extra money we need is 9 _____ the lottery, but I don't imagine that's going to happen anytime soon!

5 Replace the bold words in the sentences with words in the box so that the meaning stays the same.

| can afford | debt | ~~earnings~~ | payment |
| rate | wealth | | |

1 Every month Daniel saves 25 percent of his **money from his job**. _earnings_
2 Most students take out a student loan to pay for their college fees. This means they leave university with a **lot of money owed to the bank**.
3 The final **amount of money to pay** for my car is huge! _____
4 I don't think it's fair that only a small percentage of people own nearly all of the world's **money**. _____
5 The government are planning to put up the **amount** of income tax in the UK next year. _____
6 I'm not sure if I **have enough money** to pay for a holiday in Australia. _____

Grammar

Noun phrases 2

1 **Underline eleven noun phrases in the text.**

In Dubai in the United Arab Emirates, fighting fires has become more difficult in recent years. There are two reasons for this. One reason is the height of the buildings in the city, which makes it hard for firefighters to reach the top. Another reason is that Dubai's roads are very busy, with lots of traffic jams. Emergency fire services often find it impossible to drive traditional fire engines quickly to the site of a fire. To improve their fire services, Dubai has developed a new method of fighting fires. Instead of using the roads to get to a fire, firefighters now use the many waterways in the city. They travel along the water on jet skis to get to the fire. Then they use jetpacks on their backs to rise up into the air. The jetpack takes water from the waterway below and sends it up through the fire hose. In this way, firefighters can fight the fire from above.

2 **Find and correct five mistakes in sentences 1–8.**

seat belts

1 It doesn't seem right that buses in the UK don't have ~~seats of belts of seats~~.

2 My car engine is making a really strange noise.

3 Would you like a lift to the train station?

4 I get so angry about the rudeness of the bus drivers in this town.

5 The queue at control of passports was enormous.

6 To hire a car you need to have a licence of driving.

7 I parked the car and Mum went to get the ticket of the car park.

8 The noise traffic is deafening on Station Road.

3 **Complete the words with the correct compound nouns.**

1 when cars hit each other   c *ar*   c *rash*
2 the place where you wait for a bus   b_____ s_____
3 a place where you fill up your car with fuel   p_____ s_____
4 you use these to carry home your goods from the supermarket
s_____ b_____
5 things like trains, buses, etc   p_____ t_____
6 rules you have to follow when driving   t_____ l_____
7 organisation that will come to help you if your car has a problem
b_____ s_____
8 people who drive large vehicles as a job   l_____ d_____

Vocabulary

On the road

4 **Match the words to make compound nouns.**

1 driving —— station
2 foot ————— helmet
3 petrol ———— driver
4 flat ————— test
5 lorry ————— tyre
6 breakdown ——— path
7 motorbike ———— service

5 **Complete the sentences with the missing words.**

1 The car hit a rock and the driver lost c_____ .

2 The road goes up a hill, so it's best to drive in first or second g_____ .

3 As I was driving home last night, the car in front of me c_____ into a lamp post because the driver had fallen asleep.

4 It's illegal to ride on a motorbike without wearing a h_____ on your head.

5 Can you believe I got a one hundred euro f_____ for driving without my seat belt on?

6 I had to drive around for 15 minutes before I found somewhere to p_____ my car.

7 If I get any more p_____ on my driving licence, I won't be allowed to drive for a year.

8 The other driver said I'd p_____ o_____ in front of her, but I thought she'd signalled for me to go ahead.

9 We had to call the breakdown service when our car e_____ stopped working on the motorway.

10 The child ran in front of the lorry and the driver had to b_____ quickly.

Functional language
Deal with problems with shops and services

1 Complete the conversation with the words in the box.

> appreciate   could   helpful   nothing   me   strictly   supposed   ~~way~~

A: Hi, I bought this book here yesterday. I read the first few pages and to be honest I didn't really like it. Is there any ¹ __way__ I could get a refund?

B: Can I see your receipt please, sir?

A: Ah. No, I don't have it.

B: Well, we're not ² _____ to give refunds without a valid receipt.

A: Is there really ³ _____ you can do?

B: One second, let ⁴ _____ speak to my manager. She's just over there.

A: Thanks, I really ⁵ _____ it.

B: She says that ⁶ _____ speaking we can't give refunds without a valid receipt. So, if you could find the receipt …

A: That's the problem … I don't have it. ⁷ _____ you let me exchange if for another book, at least?

B: I'm sorry, without the receipt I can't do anything.

A: Well, thanks a lot. You've been very ⁸ _____ .

2 Put the words in the correct order to complete the answers.

1 **A:** I'm sorry, but I can't really wait two weeks for delivery.
   B: can / Let / I / see / what / me / do
   Let me see what I can do.

2 **A:** We're not supposed to allow pets in the hotel rooms, but I could let your dog stay this one time.
   B: it / really / I /appreciate
   _____

3 **A:** I'm really sorry, I don't have anyone who could fix your laptop until Monday.
   B: That's really inconvenient. there / can / nothing / Is / you / really / do / ?
   _____

4 **A:** Please could you try once more to find a table for us?
   favour / be / me / You'd / doing / huge / a
   _____
   B: Let me have a look.

5 **A:** I bought this jumper yesterday, but I've decided I don't really like it. Can I exchange it for this jacket?
   B: speak / my / me / Let / manager / to
   _____

6 **A:** That's all sorted for you now, Miss Lopez.
   B: thank / you / I / can't / enough.
   _____

Listening

1 🔊 7.01 **Listen to the conversation. Which country has Stefan visited recently?**
   a Benin   **b** Italy   **c** China   **d** Mexico

2 Listen again. Are the sentences true (T) or false (F)?
   1 Stefan got back on Sunday. _____
   2 Wuzhen is north of the Yangtze River. _____
   3 Stefan has been to Venice. _____
   4 Only tourists use vaporetti boats. _____
   5 Stefan hasn't been to Mexicaltitán in Mexico. _____
   6 Mexicaltitán is built on an island. _____
   7 Stefan has been to Ganvie in Benin. _____
   8 The people who live in Ganvie travel around in water taxis. _____

3 Listen again. Complete the sentences with the numbers from the box.

> 118   400   800   1,600   3,000   7,000

   1 Wuzhen is _____ years old.
   2 Venice has _____ separate islands.
   3 Venice is around _____ years old.
   4 Mexcaltitán is _____ metres in diameter.
   5 _____ people live in Mexcaltitán.
   6 There are about _____ buildings in Ganvie.

Reading

1 Read the texts and write the person's name next to their job.

1 vet ....
2 school nurse ....
3 accident and emergency nurse ....
4 community doctor ....
5 surgeon ....

What makes a job important and enjoyable? We asked five people who work in the health industry for their opinions.

Jemima

A Why do I do my job? Well, I feel it's a very important job. I help people when something bad happens to them. A lot of the people I see have suddenly started to feel extremely ill and they are often quite worried. These people don't have time to make an appointment with their own doctor because they need help immediately, so they come to see me. No two days are ever the same. I have patients who have nasty injuries, like a deep cut that won't stop bleeding. I also have patients who have developed very high temperatures or patients who are experiencing chest pains. I have to identify the problem, decide how bad it is and what is the best way to treat it. I like the fact that I have to make decisions all the time.

Catherine

B I do my job because I enjoy working in a small place where I know all my patients by name. I love working with children. They can come to see me when they've cut themselves badly or if they've got a stomach ache. They can be a bit sad, so I use storybooks and boxes of toys to help to make them feel better. I think that my job is really important because I talk to the children about the importance of staying healthy. I explain about good hygiene and eating habits. I think that children should understand these things in order to avoid health problems when they are adults.

Ben

C I do my job because I can't stand seeing an animal in pain. I think the fact that they can't tell you what's wrong makes my job quite difficult. A dog can't tell you that it's got a sore throat, but I can see that the dog isn't feeling well and then try to work out the reasons why. When a dog comes back to visit a week or so later, and it's happy and back to normal once more, I feel really happy.

Louise

D I do my job because I know I'm good at it. Patients come to me because their situation is very serious. They haven't just got a nasty cut or a fever. Often it's a matter of life or death, and I know that there is a chance I can help them. Although I can spend a lot of time with a patient, I won't talk to them much because they are asleep. Of course, I meet my patients before and after the operation, but not for long. I don't think I'm very good at talking to people, so I would find it hard to be a community doctor.

Yuri

E I like my job because I like helping people in my local area. I see the same patients regularly, so I get to know them and their families well. I've got some patients whose grandparents are also my patients. Sometimes the waiting room is like a social club, with people chatting and laughing while they are waiting to see me. People don't only come to see me for their health problems. I have a very sociable job. I see pregnant women and their babies, which is always lovely. Also, people come for injections before they go to interesting places abroad. I chat with my patients about lots of different things.

2 Read the texts again and answer the questions.

1 Why do patients go to see Jemima and not their usual doctor?

....
....

2 Who teaches people about how to be healthy?

....

3 Which two people mention knowing their patients well and having regular contact with them?

....

4 Which two people's patients are not adults?

....

5 What does Ben feel makes his job more difficult?

....
....

6 Who says that patients don't only see him/her because of health problems?

....

7 What reason does Louise give for not becoming a community doctor?

....
....

8 Who mentions having to make decisions?

....

9 Who says they are good at their job?

....

10 Who says their job is sociable?

....

3 Find words in the text to match definitions 1–8.

1 an arrangement to meet someone at a particular time
.... (text A)

2 people or animals who are not well and go to see the doctor/nurse/vet .... (text A)

3 the practice of keeping yourself and the things around you clean .... (text B)

4 hate .... (text C)

5 when what you do may help decide if someone lives or dies .... (text D)

6 what a surgeon does to try and fix part of someone's body .... (text D)

7 a place where people can meet and talk for pleasure
.... (text E)

8 describing someone who enjoys meeting and talking to a lot of people .... (text E)

4 Read the article. What is it about?

a the benefits of alternative therapies

b communicating well with patients

c conditions in hospitals

> Doctors, dentists and nurses train for many years to become experts in their jobs. However, a recent report says that many healthcare professionals still need help in developing a good 'bedside manner'. **1** _c_ . Doctors with a good 'bedside manner' are able to communicate well with their patients. They take time to discuss the patient's problem and how they plan to help. **2** ____ . This can help a patient to feel involved in decisions about their health problem. Evidence suggests that a good 'bedside manner' can help patients to stay calm. **3** ____ . Families usually want to be kept informed about how the patient is feeling and what treatment they are receiving. **4** ____ . They are being taught how to wear uniforms or clothes with bright colours, how to speak in a calm and friendly way, that they should sit rather than stand at a patient's bed, that they should remember to smile, and that they should ask questions about their patient's lives and interests.

5 Complete the article with sentences a–d.

a A good 'bedside manner' also involves listening to the patient, trying to understand how they feel and answering their questions.

b 'Bedside manner' is actually so important that many healthcare professionals are now receiving extra training in it.

c 'Bedside manner' means the way in which a doctor, dentist or nurse communicates with their patient.

d It also suggests that the quality of 'bedside manner' can affect patients' families, too.

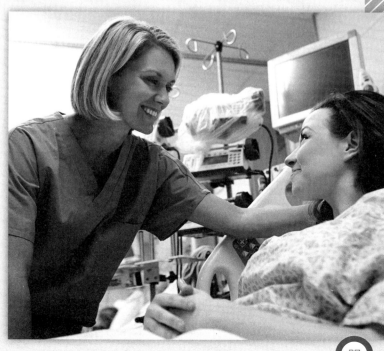

Writing

1 Read the emails quickly. Which one is formal and which is informal?

2 Read the emails again and choose the correct alternatives.

Clarence Villa

We're looking forward to welcoming you to stay at Clarence Villa. Here are the directions so that you know how to find us.

By train

When you arrive at Brighton main station, take a taxi or a bus to Clarence Villa.

Taxi: Go out of the main entrance towards the seafront and the taxis will be ¹*on/over* your left.

Bus: Go out of the main entrance towards the seafront. Walk straight ahead for about 100 metres. You should see the clock tower on your right. Turn right ²*at/in* the clock tower. You'll see a line of bus stops on the road in front of you. Take bus 74A to Kemp Town. Get ³*off/up* when you see The George pub. Clarence Villa is on the third street on the right.

By car from London, direction M23/A23

Arrive in Brighton on the A23. Follow the brown signs to the racecourse. When you get to the park (The Level), turn right and follow the edge of the park for about 300 metres. Turn left at the next set of traffic lights. Then immediately turn right ⁴*out/at* the next traffic lights. You should see St Cuthbert's Church on the left. Go all the way up the hill. At the top of the hill, turn right at the traffic lights. You should now be on Queen's Park Rd and you'll be able to see the sea ⁵*towards/ahead* of you. Go all the way to the seafront. You should be able to see Brighton Pier to the right. Turn left so that the sea is on your right-hand side. Clarence Villa is on the fourth street on your left, just ⁶*to/after* the Majestic Hotel. Please remember that you will need to buy a parking ticket for your car. The meter is about halfway ⁷*in/up* the street.

Please don't hesitate to phone if you have any difficulty with your travel arrangements.

With best wishes,
Jayne Trafford, Manager
Clarence Villas

2

Hi Sarah,

Can't wait to see you next weekend!

Don't think I've sent you directions to my new flat. The address is 34c Birch Road, London, SW15 3RS.

I assume you'll be coming ⁸*by/on* tube, so get the District Line to East Putney and leave ⁹*to/by* the main exit. If you're standing with your back to the station, then turn right and keep walking for about 200 metres. Use the subway to cross the main road. Then keep walking ¹⁰*to/in* the same direction for another 500 metres. You'll cross over a roundabout and then you'll pass a French restaurant on your left – don't stop to eat there! It's very expensive! Turn left into Soudberry Avenue and Birch Road is the third road ¹¹*on/of* the right. It's a side street, so make sure you don't miss it! As you approach, you'll see a post box ¹²*in/on* the corner! My flat is about halfway down the road, on the left. The entrance is tucked around the side. If you're facing the house, it's on your left. Just ring the top bell when you arrive! I'm right at the top of the building!

Hope this helps. Call me if you have any problems finding me!

See you on Sunday,

Tessa

3 Read the emails again. Are the sentences true (T) or false (F)?

Email 1

1 The taxis are closer than the buses to the train station. ....

2 The writer states how much a taxi costs from the station. ....

3 Clarence Villa is near the seafront. ....

4 Clarence Villa is close to a hotel. ....

5 It is not possible to park close to Clarence Villa. ....

6 The writer doesn't give directions for how to walk from the train station to Clarence Villa. ....

Email 2

7 Tessa has been living in this flat for a long time. ....

8 Tessa lives near East Putney underground station. ....

9 Sarah will pass an expensive Italian restaurant on her way to Tessa's house. ....

10 Tessa lives on a side street. ....

11 Tessa lives on the ground floor. ....

12 Sarah is visiting Tessa next Sunday. ....

4 Read the Focus box, then complete the information below with examples from the two emails.

Adding supporting details

When you give directions, you often add extra details to make sure the reader doesn't get lost.

You can give information about:

- local landmarks and easily recognised places.
  Walk straight ahead for about 100 metres until you come to a crossroads. You should see the clock tower on your right.
- distance.
  ... for about 2 kms until you see Preston Park on your left.
- facing the right way.
  Turn left so that the sea is on your right-hand side.

Email 1

local landmarks and easily recognised places

1 *seafront*

2 _____

3 _____

4 _____

distance

5 _____

6 _____

facing the right way

7 _____

8 _____

Email 2

local landmarks and easily recognised places

1 _____

2 _____

distance

3 _____

4 _____

facing the right way

5 _____

6 _____

5 Complete the sentences with the missing words.

1 Leave the airport by the main e_____ .

2 The hotel is o_____ the main road, so here are some detailed directions.

3 If you're f_____ the town hall, the conference centre is on your right.

4 When you get off the bus, keep walking in the same d_____ until you see the cinema.

5 Use the s_____ to cross under the main road, then continue straight on.

6 After about five minutes, you'll come to a big r_____ and you'll need to take the second exit.

7 We're about h_____ down Cherry Road, on the right hand side.

8 After about 100 metres, you'll come to a f_____ in the road. Take the road on the right.

9 As you a_____ the city centre, watch out for signs to the beach.

10 The hotel is on a tiny s_____ street just opposite the library.

Prepare

6 Choose one of the tasks, a or b. Make notes and plan your email.

a You are going to write an email with directions to a hotel or guest house in your town or city. Think about the following:

- where the hotel or guest house is situated
- different ways of travelling to get there
- supporting details for each way of travelling
- whether the email should be formal or informal

b A friend is visiting your new home for the first time. Think about the following:

- the reason they are coming
- where they are coming from
- the best way to get to your home
- what they should look for on their way
- what they should do if there are any problems
- whether the email should be formal or informal

Write

7 Write your email. Use the notes you made in Exercise 6 and the ideas in the Focus box to help you.

8A

Vocabulary

The environment

1 Match the sentence halves.

1 The problem with that material is that it produces   _c_
2 We have an important chemical   ....
3 We should ban vehicles which cause   ....
4 Sometimes I wonder if people really want to solve   ....
5 Some people say that we can't stop climate   ....
6 The world's natural   ....
7 One day, oil and gas are going to run   ....
8 A number of plant and animal species have died   ....

a industry in this country, which employs a lot of people.
b change, but I think we should try.
c toxic gases.
d resources are not going to last forever.
e out over the last one hundred years.
f out and we'll have to use other forms of energy.
g all the problems that we have.
h pollution and replace them with greener ones.

2 Complete the text with the words in the box.

> climate change   consuming   die out   floods
> ~~natural disasters~~   pollution   prevent   recycle
> reproducing   waste

In recent years, the number of ¹ _natural disasters_ around
the world has been increasing. For example, there have been
a lot of ² .... this year. Some scientists think
that this increase has been caused by ³ ....
We all need to try to stop this, but it's not easy. In fact, it's
a real challenge. We must look at how we behave and make
some changes. We should stop ⁴ .... so
much gas and oil. We must ⁵ .... paper,
plastic and glass, and we must look at how we get rid of
⁶ .... that we can't recycle. For example,
many tonnes of plastic end up in the oceans each year.
This ⁷ .... sometimes stops sea plants and
animals from ⁸ .... and unless we
⁹ .... this from continuing, it may eventually
cause some to ¹⁰ ....

3 Match words 1–8 with definitions a–h.

1 prevent   2 run out   3 consume   4 solve
5 natural disaster   6 reproduce   7 ~~waste~~
8 recycle

a rubbish   _7_
b find an answer to a problem   ....
c to use something again   ....
d to use something, for example fuel   ....
e to make babies, eggs or seeds   ....
f stop something from happening   ....
g an event in nature that causes damage or loss   ....
h to have no more of something   ....

Grammar

First conditional

4 Choose the correct alternatives.

1 We should recycle more things, *even if/in case* it's a
   big challenge.
2 We might slow down climate change *if/unless* everyone
   makes changes to the way we behave.
3 People in the area will need to move out of their homes
   in case/unless there's a flood.
4 Nothing is going to improve *if/unless* we do something
   about global warming now.
5 It may be too late to make any difference to climate
   change, *even if/in case* we all do everything possible.
6 Let's take the empty bottles *even if/in case* we pass a
   recycling bin on the way.
7 This species will die out *if/unless* we help to protect it.
8 We'll consume less energy *if/even if* we turn the lights
   off when we leave a room.

**5 Complete the sentences with the correct form of the
   verbs in brackets.**

1 If we use natural energy from the sun and the wind,
   we .... as much pollution.
   (not cause)
2 Even if we change our habits today, there
   .... a huge problem to solve.
   (still/be)
3 We .... the amount of carbon
   dioxide in the air if we get rid of our car. (might/reduce)
4 We .... energy if we turn off the
   computer when we're not using it. (save)
5 Some plants and animals ....
   even if we do everything we can to protect them.
   (might/die out)
6 We .... back in the house in case
   there's another earthquake. (should/not go)
7 If we all recycle more, it .... a big
   difference. (make)
8 I'll try to walk as much as possible, even if it
   .... much longer. (take)

Grammar

whatever, whoever, whenever, however, etc.

1 Put the words in the correct order to make sentences.

1 whenever / to / me / Please / you / talk / need / to
   Please talk to me whenever you need to.

2 with / Take / go / wherever / this / you / you /
   ....

3 the / Yasmin / Whatever / ready / talk / always / is / time, / to
   ....

4 nasty / him / to / me / whenever / Richard / see / is / I
   ....

5 works, / does well / However / Kamil / hard / never / he / in exams
   ....

6 goes, / her / Wherever / people / Marissa / love
   ....

7 reliable, / the situation / is / whatever / dad / My / always
   ....

8 speak / Whoever / polite / to, / be / should / you / you
   ....

2 Choose the correct option a, b or c.

1 .... you go in the world, you should try to make friends.
   a Wherever   **b** Whenever   **c** Whoever

2 Fotis always smiles .... he sees me.
   a whatever   **b** whoever   **c** whenever

3 You can't change people, ... much you want to.
   a however   **b** whatever   **c** whoever

4 Can .... borrowed my pen please return it?
   a wherever   **b** whoever   **c** whatever

5 You should do your best, ... the situation.
   a however   **b** whatever   **c** whoever

6 Try to speak the local language, ... country you're in.
   a whatever   **b** whenever   **c** wherever

7 Emilio will wait for Sandra, ... long that might be.
   a wherever   **b** however   **c** whoever

8 Give us a ring .... you're in town.
   a wherever   **b** whenever   **c** however

3 Complete the sentences with *whatever, whoever, whenever, wherever* or *however*.

1 You should always stay calm, *however* difficult that might be sometimes.

2 Ben lacks confidence .... he has to talk in public.

3 You should tell him the truth, ... happens.

4 .... he is in the world, Hari gets invited to parties.

5 You should talk to .... upset you.

6 I'll never forget you, ... much I try.

7 .... I try to call him, it goes directly to voicemail.

Vocabulary

Character

4 Complete the missing words in the sentences.

1 Tom is p *olitically* active and hopes to stand in next month's election.

2 I follow his news blog because the information is usually r........................ .

3 James was accused of being r........................ because he doesn't have any foreign workers at his company.

4 I'd like to be a comedian but I lack a bit of c........................ on stage.

5 When you disagree with someone, it's important to stay c........................ and explain your point of view.

6 My colleague is very kind and always w........................ to help me with my work.

7 I thought that Sara was nice, but she's actually a bit n........................ .

8 My brother is very b........................ . He did extremely well in his last exam.

5 Complete the text with the words in the box.

active	difficult	generous	patient	reliable	strict
~~sweet~~	talented				

I get on quite well with my family. My sister is 17 years old. She's very **1** *sweet* , so she's got a lot of friends. She's a singer in a band and she's quite **2** .... Her band is going to perform at a concert next week. However, my sister can be a bit **3** .... sometimes because she always has to get her own way.

My brother is 22. He's very politically **4** .... He works in local government and I think he wants to be president one day! He's **5** .... with his time and money, so he's got lots of friends, too.

I didn't always get on well with my dad. He's very **6** .... and when we were growing up, he didn't let us do anything. But now I've left home, we get on better.

My mum is lovely. She's **7** .... and she always listens to me whenever I need to talk. She's also very **8** ....
I know that she'll always be there for me and will never let me down.

Vocabulary

Life events

1 Match the sentence halves.

1 I'm going to take _____e_____
2 We're going to announce _____
3 We need to pay _____
4 Sue gave _____
5 They held _____
6 I've been _____
7 My partner and I live _____
8 I think that we should get married _____

a a ceremony to remember the people who died.
b in a relationship for four months now.
c together in Madrid.
d off our mortgage before we can retire.
e a year off after I graduate.
f in the spring.
g birth to a beautiful boy this morning.
h our engagement tomorrow.

2 Complete the text with the words in the box.

> birth graduated married mortgage pregnant partner
> retired together

My name is Martin and I've just
¹_____ from my job as an
architect. I've paid off my
²_____ and I'm looking forward
to spending some time with my
³_____, Jessie. I met Jessie
three years after I ⁴_____ from
university. We fell in love and
decided to start a family.
She got ⁵_____ straightaway
and gave ⁶_____ to our
daughter, Grace, in 1983. Jessie and
I have never got ⁷_____, but
we've been living ⁸_____ for
nearly 40 years now!

3 Match words 1–8 with definitions a–h and then write the correct noun form for each word.

a die   b divorce   c engaged   d graduate   e married
f pregnant   g retire   h separate

1 the end of a person or animal's life   _____a – death_____
2 the period of a person's life after they stop working _____
3 an agreement to marry someone _____
4 what happens when two people decide to live apart _____
5 the legal end of a marriage _____
6 the period when a baby grows in a female's body _____
7 the relationship between a husband and wife _____
8 a ceremony for students when they finish university _____

Grammar

Time conjunctions

4 Choose the correct alternatives.

1 *Once/ Soon* I've retired, I'm going to go travelling for a while.
2 *Until/ As soon as* he saw her, he decided he wanted to marry her.
3 I hadn't lived with a partner *until/ once* I got married.
4 *When/ Until* I've graduated, I'm going to get a job in London.
5 *Until/ After* they got married, they bought a flat.
6 I'm staying in Berlin *as soon as/ until* my graduation and then I'm going to New York.
7 Marion and Tom didn't talk to each other *after/ when* their separation.
8 Emmanuel paid off his mortgage *until/ before* he retired.

5 Complete the sentences with the correct verb or noun form of the words in brackets.

1 Josh _____arrived_____ arrived in Mexico last Monday. (arrive)
2 Sally is going to live in university accommodation until her_____ and then she'll look for a flat of her own. (graduate)
3 My parents moved abroad after they _____ from their jobs. (retire)
4 She _____ for a job after she finishes school because she wants to go travelling. (not look)
5 She felt that her life changed after she _____ her engagement. (announce)
6 They were looking forward to their wedding and starting their _____. (marry)
7 Dan is _____ to Australia as soon as he finishes his course. (move)
8 Once I _____ my mortgage, I'm going to retire. (pay off)

Functional language
Make phone calls

1 Choose the correct alternatives.

A: Hello. Thank you for ¹*call/calling* Nymans and Sons. You're ²*through/over* to Richard. ³*How/What* can I help you?

B: Hello, my name is Guy Peters. I'm ⁴*talking/ringing* about a delivery that I received from you today.

A: OK, what can we ⁵*help/do* for you?

B: I have a ⁶*difficult/problem* with some of the items that were delivered and I wondered ⁷*if/unless* I could send them back.

A: Yes, of course. Which store did the delivery come from?

B: It was the Northbrook store.

A: OK, please ⁸*hold/keep* the line while I put you through to them.

B: Thank you very much.

2 Complete the voicemails with the words in the box.

> extension   for   interested   know
> ~~reached~~   ringing   to   wondered

> Hello, you've ¹ _reached_ Pedro's Car Repair Shop. Thank you ² _____ calling. Please leave a message after the tone.

> Hello, my name is Christina Franco and I'm ³ _____ about an advert I saw in the paper for a job as a waitress. I ⁴ _____ if you could let me know if it's still available. My mobile is 07288 282 854.

> Hello, you're through ⁵ _____ Dormans and Co. If you know the ⁶ _____ number you require, please dial it now. Otherwise, hold the line to speak to an operator.

> Hello, this is Valerie Marks and I'd like to leave a message for Andrew New. I'm ⁷ _____ in the bike you advertised. I wanted to ⁸ _____ if it is still for sale. My number is 07728 282 6828

Listening

1 🔊 8.01 **Listen. What sort of conversation is this?**

  a It's a conversation between two people who work at a radio studio.

  b It's an interview with an author in a radio studio.

  c A woman has called a radio programme to give her opinion about a topic.

2 Listen again. Choose the correct option a, b or c.

1 Where and when was Maria born?

  a 1925   **b** 1950   **c** 1952

2 What nationality were her parents?

  a English and Italian   **b** English and Spanish
  c Spanish and Italian

3 Where did she go to college?

  a Italy   **b** the US   **c** the UK

4 What was the name of her first book?

  a *Irish Peaches*   **b** *Ivy's Beach*   **c** *I Risk Peace*

5 How many companies did she send her first book to?

  a more than 20   **b** just one   **c** 12

6 What was the name of her first husband?

  a Marco   **b** Paul   **c** Alex

7 How many children did she have with her first husband?

  a one   **b** two   **c** three

8 What book did she win her first prize for?

  a *Orange Marmalade*   **b** *I Win Mother's Day*
  c *A Range of Memories*

3 Listen again and answer the questions.

1 Why does Maria love words and language?

2 Why does she love books?

3 Why did she take a year off after graduation?

4 Why does Maria think that so many publishers said no to her first book?

5 Why has Maria stayed with the same publishing company?

6 Why didn't she have much time to write in her early thirties?

7 Why are Maria's later books more serious than her early books?

8 Why was winning a prize a turning point in Maria's life?

Reading

1 **Read the magazine article and choose the best title.**

a How to improve your relationship with your boss

b How to communicate in relationships

c How to be a good friend

2 **Read the questionnaire and answer the questions.**

3 **Read the questionnaire again. Are the sentences true (T) or false (F)?**

1 This questionnaire will help you understand how your friends behave. ......

2 The first question is about what you would do if you saw racist behaviour. ......

3 The second question is about what you would do if you saw your boss bullying someone. ......

4 The third question is about whether you make time for people who may be lonely. ......

5 The fourth question is about a communication problem with a friend. ......

6 The fifth question is about how you can improve a relationship with a relative. ......

7 There are questions about relationships with partners, friends, family and people you work with. ......

8 The questionnaire has been written by scientists. ......

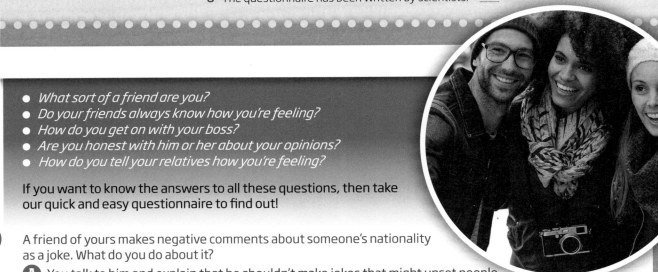

- *What sort of a friend are you?*
- *Do your friends always know how you're feeling?*
- *How do you get on with your boss?*
- *Are you honest with him or her about your opinions?*
- *How do you tell your relatives how you're feeling?*

If you want to know the answers to all these questions, then take our quick and easy questionnaire to find out!

1 A friend of yours makes negative comments about someone's nationality as a joke. What do you do about it?

Ⓐ You talk to him and explain that he shouldn't make jokes that might upset people.

Ⓑ You talk to the rest of your friends and find a way of talking to him about it together.

Ⓒ You do nothing about it. Whatever he said, it's none of your business.

2 Your boss has become politically active, but all her conversations are about politics now and it's starting to annoy the employees. What do you do about it?

Ⓐ You talk to her and explain that she should talk about other things, not just politics.

Ⓑ Whenever she talks about politics, you change the subject and hope she gets the message.

Ⓒ You let her talk about whatever she wants.

3 An elderly relative, who lives alone, phones you just as you're going out to meet a friend. You don't really have time to talk to him. What do you do?

Ⓐ You explain that you can't talk to him and put the phone down.

Ⓑ You listen for a while, but then explain that you have to go and promise to phone him back later.

Ⓒ You let him talk for as long as he likes.

4 A friend suddenly stops answering your text messages and emails. What do you do about it?

Ⓐ You phone her and ask her what's wrong.

Ⓑ You talk to other friends to find out if they know what's upset her.

Ⓒ You stop sending her messages. She'll get over it and call you when she's ready.

5 You have a difficult relationship with your mother-in-law, which upsets your partner. How can you make the situation better?

Ⓐ You go and see your mother-in-law and try to work out a way you can get on better.

Ⓑ You set up a family meeting with your partner and mother-in-law to try to discuss the situation.

Ⓒ You avoid your mother-in-law whenever you can.

Now read the results. We may not be scientists, but we can tell you a bit more about what your answers say about you!

4 Read the results of the questionnaire below. Match paragraphs 1–3 with headings a–c.

  a Mostly As   **b** Mostly Bs   **c** Mostly Cs

1 .... :
You don't like to disagree with people, so you avoid these situations. This means that you are easy to get on with and you hardly ever have arguments with your friends. People probably don't know anything about how you're feeling though. You should try to be honest with others about important things.

2 .... :
You always say what you think in your relationships, even when you disagree with someone. This is good because people will always know how you feel. Be careful that you don't upset people by being difficult, though. Sometimes, you should think about how other people feel.

3 .... :
You try to let people know how you feel in relationships and you always do it in a way that won't upset them. You are kind because you think about others. But people might not always understand how you're really feeling. You should have a bit more confidence when you talk to others.

5 Read the comments. Do you think these people would answer Mostly As, Mostly Bs or Mostly Cs?

1
> I like to be honest about the way I'm feeling, but I hate having arguments. I'll often try and find a way of communicating my message without saying it in a way that might upset someone.

2
> I think you should be honest, whatever you have to say. That's what I always do and I don't care if I upset people along the way.

3
> I like an easy life. That generally means I stay away from trouble. I don't always say what's on my mind, but everyone else is usually too busy talking to listen anyway!

6 Match the words in the box with definitions 1–8.

| argument | avoid | hardly ever | honest | mostly | opinion |
| relative | upset | | | | |

1 almost all or almost always ....
2 point of view ....
3 almost never ....
4 someone in your family ....
5 to make someone feel worried or unhappy ....
6 to choose not to do something ....
7 always telling the truth ....
8 a conversation where you disagree with someone ....

8

Writing

1 Read the four texts. Which of them contain more formal language?

2 Use phrases and sentences 1–4 to complete texts A–D.

1 Of course I'll come!
2 Thank you very much for the invitation to Richard and Hannah's wedding.
3 It's going to be a simple wedding.
4 The wedding will take place at the following address:

A

Invitation

You are warmly invited to the wedding of

RICHARD DAVISON
and
HANNAH STEPHENS

1 _____

Southsea Registry Office
on 20 September at 3 p.m.

Dinner will be served afterwards at
Grates Restaurant,
34 High St, Southsea.

Dress code: formal
RSVP by 13 June to Mr and Mrs Stephens,
14 Western Road, Southsea.
Should you have any special dietary requirements,
please advise in your reply.

B

Dear Mr and Mrs Stephens,

__³___ . This is a note to confirm that I will be attending. I don't eat meat, so I would appreciate a vegetarian meal.

Best wishes,
Saira Filfil

C

Hi Saira,

I said yes!!!! Can you believe it? I'm getting married!

You must have had your formal invitation by now, but I thought I'd drop you a quick line and say how much I'd like it if you can come to the wedding.

2 _____ Just a quick ceremony at the local registry office, then we'll have dinner at a nice restaurant afterwards. If there's anything you don't eat, then just let me know.

Lots of love,

Hannah

X

D

Hi Hannah!

WOW!! CONGRATULATIONS! I'm so happy for you!
And thank you so much for inviting me! **4** _____ . Nothing could keep me away! I'm still a vegetarian, so no meat for me, please.

Really looking forward to it and hope to see you before the big day!

Love as ever,

Saira

---

3 Read the Focus box and then find formal or informal phrases in the texts that mean the same as phrases 1–5 below.

Formal and informal language

Formal	Informal
Clear layout and design headings underlining bullets (•)	**Text** (no obvious layout)
No contractions *You are*	**Contractions** *I'm We'll*
More passives **(fewer *I* and *we*)** *You are warmly invited*	**More direct (*I/We*)** *I said yes!!!!!* *We'll have dinner*
Other more formal grammar (*will/would/should*) *The marriage will* take place *Should you* have any special dietary requirements.	**More everyday grammar** It's *going to be* a simple wedding *If there's anything you don't eat, then just let me know.*
Formal words *RSVP confirm* *appreciate*	**Usual words** *let me know so happy* *Of course I'll come!*

1 We'll have dinner _____ (text A)
2 Thanks for inviting me! _____ (text B)
3 Should you have any special dietary requirements _____ (text C)
4 I'd be delighted to attend. _____ (text D)
5 I'm afraid I don't eat meat. _____ (text D)

4 Choose the correct alternatives in this formal invitation.

> [1]*You are warmly invited/We invite you* to the Haymans & Sons summer party on 18 May.
> [2]*The summer party is held/We have a party* each year to celebrate the success of the business.
> [3]*Drinks will be served/You will get a drink* at 6.30 p.m. and
> [4]*we'll have dinner at/dinner will start* at 7.30 p.m.
> Dress code: [5]*formal/wear smart clothes*
> [6]*If you need/Should you require* any specific access, then please [7]*include this in your RSVP/let me know*.
> [8]*RSVP/get back to me by* 14 March.

5 Choose the correct option a, b or c.
1 All award winners will _____ a special gift bag.
   a hold   b seize   c receive
2 The event will be _____ by the town mayor.
   a guested   b hosted   c owned
3 You are _____ invited to the wedding of Ryan and Jenny.
   a warm   b warmly   c coldly
4 _____ you require transport to the reception, contact Peter.
   a Could   b Would   c Should
5 You are invited to _____ the awards ceremony on 3 September.
   a attend   b attach   c attract
6 The launch party will be _____ at the golf course.
   a made   b held   c produced
7 This is a note to _____ that I will be attending the wedding.
   a confirm   b confess   c conflict
8 I don't eat meat, so I would _____ a vegetarian meal.
   a demand   b expect   c appreciate

6 Match the sentence halves.
1 You are warmly invited to the   __e__
2 Should you have any special   _____
3 RSVP by: _____
4 The event will take   _____
5 A light dinner and drinks   _____
6 Dress code: _____

a 5 June
b casual
c place at St Leonard's Town Hall.
d will be served.
e Golden Anniversary of Tom and Tina Brookman.
f requests, please advise in your reply.

Prepare

7 You are going to write a formal invitation to a wedding anniversary party. Think about:
- where and when the party will take place
- other useful information about the party
- how you would like the person invited to respond
- the date when you would like them to respond by

Write

8 Write your invitation. Then write a formal acceptance to the invitation. Use your notes from Exercise 7 and the ideas in the Focus box to help you.

Vocabulary

Quality of life

1 **Match the sentence halves.**

1 Sometimes life is difficult, but I know that my family have faith _g_

2 It's so sad that some people still face _____

3 It takes me a while to trust _____

4 We need a stronger _____

5 I don't like to talk about all the work I do _____

6 There isn't a lot of violence here, but there's _____

7 I think these days there is more tolerance _____

8 Social media creates pressure to show how interesting _____

a of different lifestyles, but the situation is still not perfect.

b quite a lot of less serious crime.

c our lives are, which can cause a lot of anxiety.

d community here; people don't even know who their neighbours are.

e for charity. That's not why I do it.

f new people, but when I do, I can be a great friend.

g in me, and that helps me continue.

h discrimination because of their age, gender or race.

2 **Complete the text with the words in the box.**

> ~~communities~~   discrimination   fact of life   generous
> part-time   pressure   spaces   tolerance   violence
> wages

Many people believe that quality of life was much better in the UK in the 1950s and 1960s. Our image is that everyone lived in strong **1** _communities_ surrounded by friends and family. We imagine children playing safely in the streets or in wonderful green **2** _____ in the sunshine. We think that there was no crime or **3** _____ and that everybody felt safe at any time of the day or night.

There was less of a consumer culture, so people felt less **4** _____ to buy the latest clothes, cars or electronic items. We also have the idea that everyone was very **5** _____, helping each other all the time and doing lots for charity. In short, we think that happiness was just a **6** _____ in the 1950s and 1960s. Was this really true?

Not completely. Men often had jobs with good **7** _____, but women usually stayed at home or worked **8** _____. There was less equality and people from different backgrounds often faced **9** _____. Most people agree that today, there is greater **10** _____ of people different from ourselves.

Grammar

Patterns after *wish*

3 **Put the words in the correct order to make sentences.**

1 I / to / part-time / work / wish / could / afford / I
   I wish I could afford to work part-time.

2 police / wish / more / I / there / on / streets / our / were
   _____

3 we / afford / move / could / to / We / wish
   _____

4 I / they / wish / collect / rubbish / more often / would / the
   _____

5 work / weekends / I / didn't / wish / have to / Noor
   _____

6 people / I / weren't / rude / so / wish
   _____

7 to / I / I / didn't / go / work / today / have to / wish
   _____

8 traffic jam / would / I / move / wish / this
   _____

4 **Choose the correct alternatives.**

1 I wish I *work/ worked* for a charity.

2 I wish my teacher *would/ could* speak more slowly.

3 I wish my neighbours *would/ were* turn the music down.

4 I wish I *would/ could* visit my parents more often.

5 I wish I *live/ lived* in a smaller town.

6 I wish I *can/ could* come with you to Greece.

7 I wish I *had/ could* time to go to the gym today.

8 I wish James *would/ will* message me.

5 **Rewrite the sentences using *I wish*.**

1 There's a party tonight. I want to go, but I can't.
   I wish I could go to the party tonight.

2 All the benches in the park are broken. I'd like the council to mend them.
   _____

3 I don't know what to do.
   _____

4 There aren't enough trains. The train company really needs to put more on.
   _____

5 I'd like to have my own car, but I don't.
   _____

6 There are no streetlights by the beach. I think there should be.
   _____

7 I'd like to be able to help Ollie, but I can't.
   _____

8 The weather is so cold and wet. I'd like it to be hot and sunny.
   _____

Vocabulary

Society

1 Match words 1–10 with definitions a–j.

1 chaos 2 ~~democracy~~ 3 fund 4 peace 5 poverty

6 racism 7 rights 8 state 9 wealth 10 vote

a a political system where people choose their government by voting for it _2_

b when there is no order or organisation ....

c a large amount of money or property ....

d when people are very poor ....

e the belief that people of some races are inferior to people of other races ....

f the government of a country ....

g when things are quiet and calm ....

h things that people should be able to do or have ....

i a choice in an election ....

j provide the money for something ....

2 Choose the correct alternatives to complete the text.

HOME > News > Latest

Power struggle in Bartholomew

RM NEWS – 1 hour ago

Police officials admit that drug gangs have completely ¹*taken/turned* over the Bartholomew area of the city. After several days of fighting, reports say that the police lost control at about 4.30 a.m. this morning. The area is now being ²*ruled/regulated* by gang members and the police have no authority there. Yesterday evening, the police advised inhabitants to leave the area, but the ³*most/majority* of people decided to stay. All this morning, gang members have been driving around the city disturbing the ⁴*peace/process* and the community is angry that they are having to ⁵*place/put* up with this. People are demanding that the police get ⁶*rule/rid* of the gangs. Bartholomew is an area of intense poverty, with high levels of unemployment and many ⁷*houseless/homeless* people. There is a large problem with health, as most people cannot afford ⁸*hospital care/healthcare*. Many young people sell drugs for the gang in order to be able to ⁹*fund/free* a trip to see a doctor.

💬 Like

Grammar

Second conditional

3 Match the sentence halves.

1 If I wasn't a teacher, ___c___

2 We might have more money, ...

3 What would you say ....

4 If you could change one thing in the world, ...

5 If there was no government, ...

6 If people walked everywhere, ...

7 It would end poverty ....

8 If we made robots cleverer than humans, ...

a if someone asked you to rule the country?

b there would be chaos.

c I'd like to be a politician.

d if we all earned the same wage.

e they might take over the world.

f if we didn't go out so much.

g it could solve our environmental problems.

h what would it be?

4 Find and correct the mistakes in each sentence.

have

1 If people didn't /~~had to~~ work, they would get very bored.

2 If you would be a millionaire, what would you spend your money on?

3 What will you do if you lost your job?

4 If I would write the *Hunger Games*, I would be a very rich woman now.

5 If I had a better imagination, I must be able to imagine a world like that.

6 If I lived in a world ruled by robots, I fight to take control.

7 I might think I was dreaming if I wake up to find that everyone in society was equal.

8 What rules you make if you were asked to create a perfect society?

9c

Grammar
Past modals of deduction

1 Complete the sentences with *must, might* or *can't*.

1 There's no way he won fairly. He ___*must*___ have cheated in the race.
2 I've lost my phone. I _____ have left it on the bus or I suppose it could be at work. I just don't know!
3 She _____ have competed in the last Olympics because she wasn't good enough.
4 The shops _____ have been empty in town, because everyone was watching the final.
5 Gordal hasn't moved yet. She _____ have heard the starting whistle.
6 The fans _____ have been delighted with that amazing score.
7 The losing team's journey home _____ have been much fun.
8 The players are still continuing to play, so they _____ have seen the dog on the pitch.

2 Correct the words in bold in the conversations.

1 A: My girlfriend ran the marathon last weekend.
   must
   B: Wow! You ¹**might** have been so proud of her.
   A: Yes, I was. She did it with a bad knee, too.
   B: Really? That ²**must** have been easy!
   A: It wasn't! But she did really well. She completed the marathon in seven hours.
   B: That's good, she ³**can't** have been pleased with that time.

2 A: Hey, Jules, congratulations on doing the marathon at the weekend. It ⁴**might** have been exhausting!
   B: It was.
   A: You ⁵**might** have been really pleased to finish.
   B: Yes, but I wasn't very pleased with my time. I was quite slow. I ⁶**must** have done better if I'd trained more.

Vocabulary
Sport

3 Write the words and phrases in the box in the correct columns in the table below.

> break the record time   ~~come last~~   get beaten
> get knocked out   get sent off   in the lead
> miss a penalty

positive	negative
	come last

4 Match the sentence halves.

1 He missed a ___*b*___
2 Paola became a black _____
3 Last year, our country got to _____
4 That horse was _____
5 It's amazing how athletes continue to break _____
6 Sofia has been chosen to represent _____
7 She fell _____
8 The match wasn't a fair _____

a her country in the women's volleyball.
b penalty in the World Cup final.
c the quarter-finals.
d the favourite to win the race.
e world records.
f contest because one of the teams had a couple of injured players.
g belt in karate two years ago.
h over just as she was about to score.

5 Complete the sentences with the correct form of the verbs in the box.

> break   come last   drown   get beaten   send   train

1 James nearly _____ when his boat got damaged in the race.
2 The football team _____ six days a week.
3 The referee _____ the player off the pitch for dangerous behaviour.
4 I didn't do well in the race. I _____ by ten other people who were faster.
5 Webster failed to _____ the record time in this race.
6 Issa was disappointed that he didn't win his race but at least he didn't _____ .

9D

Functional language
Interrupt politely

1 Complete the conversation with the words in the box.

about   back   ~~could~~   go   interrupt   mind   point
worries

A: OK. We've been thinking about the new project. We would like Priya to be the project manager, with Ulla working as her assistant.

B: Which means that Ted will need to co-ordinate with Priya and Fred will need to co-ordinate with Rachel.

A: Exactly, and …

C: I'm sorry, but ¹ _could_ I just stop you there for a moment?

A: Of course.

C: Sorry, but would you ² _____ just repeating that?

B: Don't worry, it's all on page five of the handout.

C: Great. Sorry ³ _____ that. Please ⁴ _____ on.

A: No ⁵ _____ . So, to get ⁶ _____ to what I was saying. We've still got to assign a project manager to the Yaleberg project.

B: I think Fred could do it.

A: Good idea.

C: Sorry to ⁷ _____ you again, but will Fred have enough time?

B: That's a fair ⁸ _____ . Let's discuss with him.

2 Put the words in the correct order to complete the conversation.

A: ¹I / say / could / something / just / there ?
Could I just say something there?

B: Yes, of course.

A: ²just / I / Sorry / make / suggestion / to / but / wanted / quick / a
_____ . That's probably not going to happen because the trains don't go through Waterloo on a Sunday. It might be better to meet at Victoria.

B: You're right. ³out / Thanks / pointing / for / that
_____

A: Yes. ⁴interrupt / sorry / to / Anyway,
_____

B: No worries. ⁵I / So, / saying / as / was
_____ . How about if we meet at 7 p.m. at Victoria and then get a taxi to the Southbank?

A: ⁶mind / Do / if / here / you / I / come / in ?

B: No, of course not.

A: Thanks. I just think it might be quicker to go by underground. ⁷saying / you / were / So ?

B: Yes, so we'll meet at Victoria and go to the Southbank by underground.

A: ⁸stop / there / moment / Could / I / a / just / you / for ?

B: Yes, what it is now … ?

9

Listening

1 🔊 9.01 Listen to the radio programme. What is it about?

a how to train young children to be footballers

b the best way to develop young children into sporting successes

c why some of our top sporting stars are successful

2 Listen again. Tick (✓) the statements Dr Ramiresh agrees with.

1 Training children in one sport from a young age can have a negative effect on their physical development. ✓

2 Children need to focus on the sports they are good at.

3 Free play is good for young children.

4 If young children only learn one sport, they will not learn all the physical skills they need.

5 Even if children are talented at a sport, they shouldn't be encouraged to play it.

6 Teenagers can begin to focus on one particular sport.

7 Children who are pushed hard often become sporting successes.

8 Children need to be told what they have done wrong.

3 Listen again and choose the correct option a or b.

1 What is Dr Ramiresh's job?
a child sports psychologist   **b** sports star

2 What is the name of Dr Ramiresh's book?
a 'Called Free'   **b** 'Free to Play'

3 What age does he consider too young to start training children in sports?
a one or two   **b** three or four

4 Dr Ramiresh says that using lots of different play and sporting equipment helps young children to develop in two ways. What are these?
a their strength and flexibility
b their movement skills and their co-ordination.

5 What is Dr Ramiresh's definition of 'free play'?
a play with no rules
b play you don't have to pay for

6 Who does the presenter say would disagree with Dr Ramiresh's view that young children shouldn't focus on just one sport?
a sports coaches   **b** talented sports stars

7 Dr Ramiresh says that children who are pushed too hard can become sporting failures. When can this happen?
a their teenage years   **b** their twenties

8 What sort of health issues does he say that many of these children suffer from as adults?
a mental health issues   **b** physical issues

Reading

1 **Read the article. Who is it about?**
a Thomas More
b Nuño Beltrán de Guzmán
c Vasco de Quiroga

2 **Read the text again and match headings 1–5 to paragraphs A–E.**
1 Creating a Utopia _E_
2 Vasco de Quiroga's arrival in Mexico ....
3 A desire to change things ....
4 Starting again ....
5 An early example of Utopia ....

Real-life Utopia

Statue of Vasco de Quiroga in Michoacán

A Many people say that Utopia cannot exist. They say that it is a **dream** that can never come true. However, there are people who have tried to create Utopian societies, in which everyone has their own purpose and is valued by others. One of the earliest examples was in the 16th century, when a man called Vasco de Quiroga created a Utopia in Mexico.

B Vasco de Quiroga was born in the 15th century in Spain. His family was wealthy and he trained to be a lawyer. As Quiroga got older, he decided to become a priest. In 1531, when he was in his sixties, he travelled to Mexico, where the Spanish conquistadors had taken control. The conquistadors had destroyed many Mexican communities. They had taken people's wealth and **forced** them to live in poverty.

C The cruel conquistador, Nuño Beltrán de Guzmán was in charge of western Mexico. There was **chaos** everywhere. Quiroga disagreed with the methods Guzmán used. He had read Thomas More's book *Utopia* and he agreed with More's ideas. He believed that instead of **mistreating** the Mexican people, it would be more helpful to give them a way to earn wages.

D Over the years, Guzmán had made many enemies and people came from Spain to arrest him. He tried to **escape** from Mexico after he had destroyed an area called Michoacán. However, Guzmán was finally caught and taken to Spain, where he was put in prison for the rest of his life. At this time, Mexico was in a terrible condition, and in 1532 Quiroga used his own money to build a hospital-school in Michoacán.

E In 1537, Quiroga became Bishop of Michoacán. He felt he had the **opportunity** to try to build More's Utopia in Michoacán. He helped to build communities and provided people with education in religion and the arts. Each community was taught a different art, so that they could learn the best techniques. Communities were encouraged to sell what they had made to other communities. Also, Quiroga divided up the land so that each family had their own house and land for growing vegetables and keeping animals. He built schools, hospitals, churches and even the first university in the **region**. Perhaps most importantly, Quiroga taught people how they could rule themselves. People throughout Mexico **appreciated** what Quiroga did for them, and many Mexicans still call him the 'father' of Michoacán.

3 Are the sentences true (T) or false (F)? Correct the false sentences.

1 The *conquistadores* were Mexican. ....

2 Vasco de Quiroga was born in the 15th century. ....

3 Quiroga was Mexican. ....

4 Quiroga came from a poor family. ....

5 Nuño Beltrán de Guzmán treated the Mexicans badly. ....

6 Quiroga disagreed with the ideas in Thomas More's book *Utopia*. ....

7 Guzmán died in Mexico. ....

8 Guzmán gave Quiroga money to build a hospital-school in Michoacán. ....

4 Complete the sentences with one, two or three words from the text.

1 One of the first Utopian societies was created in .... (paragraph A)

2 The conquistadors destroyed many Mexican .... (paragraph B)

3 Vasco de Quiroga trained to be a .... (paragraph B)

4 Quiroga did not go to Mexico until he was .... (paragraph B)

5 Quiroga .... Guzmán methods of controlling the Mexican people. (paragraph C)

6 The first thing that Quiroga built in Michoacán was a .... (paragraph D)

7 Quiroga started building his Utopia when he became .... (paragraph E)

8 Quiroga built lots of things, such as churches, a university, ... and .... (paragraph E)

5 Match the words in bold in the article with definitions 1–8.

1 were thankful for ....

2 to be made to do something you don't want to do ....

3 a chance to do something ....

4 a hope or ambition ....

5 treat someone badly ....

6 run away ....

7 when everything is happening in a confused way and nothing is organised ....

8 an area of a country ....

6 Read the three definitions of Utopia below. Which one is most similar to Vasco de Quiroga's version of Utopia?

a I think in a Utopia we would all be able to do exactly what we wanted to do, whatever made us happy.

Mel, 34

b For a Utopia to actually work, I think you would need to choose which people to include and send all the others away.

Asman, 25

c In a Utopia, everyone has to have a purpose and everyone has to value each other's contribution to that society.

Jane, 23

7 Read the text and choose the correct text type.

a book review   b film review   c theatre review

Avatar was first seen in cinemas in 2009, but it's still my favourite science-fiction film. It's set on an alien moon called Pandora, where people called the Na'vi live. Everyone works together in this Utopian society. They love the land and they don't try to control the animals. They ask permission to ride or fly on them.

Every time I watch the film, I find the idea of Pandora even more beautiful. The film shows future people from Earth as very selfish. They don't care about each other, about the Na'vi people or about Pandora. They try to take over Pandora and to control the Na'vi.

What I love the most in the film is the love story between Neytiri, the Na'vi princess, and Jake Sully. Jake is a US soldier who is sent to Pandora to find out about the Na'vi people. He soon realises that what people from Earth want to do to Pandora is wrong, and he does what he can to try to help the Na'vi.

8 Read the text again and answer the questions.

1 What is the name of the film?
....

2 When was it first shown in cinemas?
....

3 Where is the Utopian society located?
....

4 Who are the Na'vi?
....

5 How do the Na'vi treat animals on Pandora?
....

6 How does the writer describe the people from Earth?
....

7 What does the writer love the most about the film?
....

8 What is Jake's job?
....

Writing

1 Read the blog post. Why do you think it was written?

   a The writer wants to invite people to attend a wedding party, and is giving some interesting information about the couple.

   b The writer is very proud of his relatives, and wants to share their story.

   c The writer wants to show how difficult life can be for older people and ask people to help.

2 Read the blog post again. Choose the correct alternatives.

Billy
1 hour

Congratulations to my grandmother, who is getting married today! Everyone is so happy for her, **1**_because/ due to_ we know what a difficult couple of years she's had.

For anyone who's missed Granny May's story, here it is!

Two years ago, Granny May caught a virus and got so sick **2**_that/since_ she had to move in with her daughter and son-in-law. **3**_As a result/Due to_, she couldn't see her friends and neighbours as often as she used to. Granny May became quite lonely and depressed. One day, after Granny May had started to recover, she saw an advert asking for people to volunteer in the local charity shop. **4**_As/So_ Granny May rang the number and soon afterwards she started working at the shop two days a week. She really enjoyed working there because she liked helping the charity and it was a great chance to meet new people.

At the charity shop, she met Ralph, who also worked there. Ralph is a very kind man who used to be a school teacher until he retired eight years ago. After a couple of months, Ralph asked Granny May to go out for afternoon tea with him. However, **5**_because/that_ it had snowed, they had to cancel their date. The weather was really bad for a long time after that, **6**_since/so_ it was two months later before Ralph and May actually saw each other again. **7**_That/Since_ they couldn't meet up, Granny May and Ralph FaceTimed each other on their computers every day. They talked about everything in their lives. **8**_As a result/ Due to_ they fell in love! Ralph asked May to marry him, and she agreed. Everyone was surprised – but delighted to hear their news

Today is their wedding day. Hurray! I'll post a full description of the day and lots of photographs later!

3 Read the blogpost again and answer the questions.

   1 Who is getting married today?

   2 Why did Granny May move in with her daughter and son-in-law?

   3 Why did Granny May become lonely and depressed?

   4 How did she find out about volunteering at the local charity shop?

   5 How much time did she spend working at the charity shop?

   6 Why did Granny May and Ralph have to cancel their date to have afternoon tea?

   7 How long was it before they saw each other again after that?

   8 How did they speak to each other during the winter?

4 Read the Focus box. Then underline the result clause in the sentences below.

Expressing cause and effect

There are many ways you can express cause and result.

Cause	Result
The tickets were so expensive	*(**that**) we decided not to go.*
It's a very popular event,	***so** you should book soon.*
***Since** I was working near the stadium,*	*I went to queue up for tickets.*
***Because/As** it was so crowded,*	*we couldn't see a thing.*
***Due to** the bad weather,*	*they cancelled the match.*
The crowds had become dangerous.	***As a result**, they've moved the carnival out of the city.*

Result	Cause
It was amazing	***because** no-one expected her to win!*
It was cancelled	***due to** a lack of interest.*
I missed her wedding	***because of** illness.*

---

1 It was terrible because no one could get to work.
2 Because it was a winter wedding, we all wore coats.
3 Mum hurt her foot dancing, so Dad had to carry her to the car.
4 Due to the age of most of the guests, the party ended at 10 p.m.
5 As Aunty Jackie was on holiday, she wasn't at the wedding.
6 Granny May looked amazing because she'd had her hair and makeup done professionally.
7 Ralph couldn't hear anything due to an ear infection.
8 Since Granny May hasn't got her own home, they're going to live in Ralph's house.

5 Match the sentence halves.

1 Dan and Sarah were so in love   *c*
2 They sent out invitations early, ...
3 Since they'd already been together for three years, ...
4 Because they don't have a lot of money, ...
5 Due to illness, ...
6 It was a great day ....

a they decided to have a short engagement.
b Sarah and Dan aren't going on honeymoon.
c that they decided to get married.
d so that their guests could save the date.
e because everyone was happy for the bride and groom.
f her grandmother couldn't come.

6 Rewrite the sentences using the words in brackets.

1 The tickets were expensive, so we decided not to go. (that)
   The tickets were so expensive that we decided not to go.

2 The weather conditions were dangerous, so the schools were closed. (due)
   _____
   _____

3 They changed the wedding venue to another place because it was so small. (as)
   _____
   _____

4 Because the demand was so high, the show sold out quickly. (because of)
   _____
   _____

5 Since they were so tired, they decided not to join the rest of the group. (that)
   _____
   _____

6 Due to the cancelled flight, she had to stay in Napoli an extra night. (as)
   _____
   _____

7 Because they had never met before, they were a little shy with each other. (since)
   _____
   _____

8 As the weather was so hot, they decided not to go outside. (due)
   _____
   _____

Prepare

7 You're going to write a social media post describing how two people you know (real or imagined) got to know each other. Think about the following:
- where and when they met
- why they were both in the same place
- anything that was unusual about how they got to know each other
- why their story is interesting

Write

8 Write your social media post using your ideas from Exercise 7 and the Focus box to help you.

Vocabulary
Influential people

1 Match words 1–10 with definitions a–j.

   1 activist   **2** athlete   **3** architect

   4 ~~explorer~~   **5** poet   **6** lawyer

   7 military leader   **8** painter

   9 philosopher   **10** trade union leader

   a someone who travels to and finds out about new places   _4_

   b someone who writes poems   ....

   c someone who takes part in activities to encourage social or political change   ....

   d someone who creates pictures   ....

   e someone who studies and gives their opinions about the meaning of life   ....

   f someone who gives advice about the law   ....

   g someone who is the head of an army   ....

   h someone who is trained in a particular sport and takes part in competitions   ....

   i someone who designs new buildings   ....

   j someone who represents people who work in a particular industry   ....

2 Complete the sentences using the words in the box.

> defended   designed   gold medals   sailing
> right   victories   widely read   works

   1 Akbar the Great (1542–1605) was the third Moghul emperor of India. He was a great military leader and had many .... in battle against the Afghans.

   2 Ben Ainslie from is the most successful Olympic sailor ever. He won four .... in the Olympic Games plus a silver.

   3 Architect Adrian Smith .... the world's tallest building (so far), The Burj Khalifa in Dubai.

   4 The Salvador Dali Museum in Florida has the largest collection outside Europe of Dali's .... of art.

   5 Activist and human rights lawyer, Amal Clooney, has .... many high-profile clients during her work.

   6 In 2017, French sailor Francois Gabart beat the existing world record for .... around the world on his own. He was able to do this six days faster than the previous world record.

   7 The 'suffragette' movement in the UK fought for women's .... to vote.

   8 Charles Dickens, who wrote *Oliver Twist*, has always been incredibly popular. He has to be one of the most .... authors of all time.

Grammar
Third conditional

3 Choose the correct alternatives.

   1 If I *hadn't been/ didn't go* there, I wouldn't *have believed/ hadn't believed* what happened.

   2 If the suffragette movement *never exists/ had never existed*, women *won't be/ might never have been* allowed to vote.

   3 If she *would work/ had worked* harder, *she would have passed/ had passed* her exams.

   4 If *I had been/ was* good at art, I *would have studied/ had studied* painting at college.

   5 I *wouldn't read/ might not have read* this book if I *didn't go/ hadn't gone* into the bookshop to get out of the rain.

   6 I *might have studied/ study* philosophy in the evenings if I *had had/ have* enough free time.

   7 If my grandmother *didn't miss/ hadn't missed* her train home, she would *never meet/ have met* my grandfather.

4 Complete the text with the correct form of the verbs in brackets to make third conditional sentences.

> **Architect Jørn Utzon**
>
> Jørn Utzon is famous because he was the architect who designed the iconic Sydney Opera House. If Utzon **1** _had followed_ (follow) his original dream of designing boats, he **2** .... (never design) this famous building. Utzon studied architecture and graduated in 1942. In 1956, there was a competition in Sydney for the design of a new opera house. If they **3** .... (not have) a competition, Utzon **4** .... (would never get) this important job. Utzon's designs for the opera house were very difficult to follow. If the designs **5** .... (not be) so complicated, they **6** .... (would/not spend) so much money on the project. In 1966, Utzon left the project, and he wasn't able to finish the building. This was good news for architect Peter Hall, who **7** .... (would/never work) on the Sydney Opera House if Utzon **8** .... (not left). This story does have a happy ending though, because Utzon received the Pritzker Architecture Prize in 2003. He **9** .... (may never win) this prize if he **10** .... (not design) the Sydney Opera House!

Vocabulary
Successes and failures

1 Match the sentence halves.

1 In my previous job I was responsible ....
2 Lucas never volunteers to help ....
3 When my boss talked about reorganising the department, he attracted ....
4 Yolanda's really upset because she got a low ....
5 We need more time, so could we ....
6 I heard you had ....
7 I'm disappointed with Kyle because he never meets ....
8 No one in the class achieved ....

a grade for the project.
b a disagreement with Paul. Everything OK?
c delay the meeting until next week?
d for bringing in new clients.
e the mark they wanted.
f a lot of opposition.
g unless he gains something from it.
h his deadlines.

2 Complete the email with words in the box.

> action deadline forced introduce manage
> opposition results rush situation standard
> task volunteered

● ● ●

Dear Graham,

Thank you for sending through your report. I appreciate that you have sent it before the **1**........................ of the 30th July. However, in my opinion, you have written the report in a **2**........................ . As a result, I think it is not of the required high **3**........................ that we were expecting. As you know, this was a very important report and as you **4**........................ for the **5**........................ , I thought that you could **6**........................ to do it. I can see now that you couldn't. This now puts me in a very difficult **7**........................ as I must present this report in an important meeting on Monday. As you know, the idea in this report has already attracted a lot of **8**........................ from various managers, so it is very important that we are clear about how we are going to **9**........................ the new plan. I don't think you have explained the process at all well. You also haven't mentioned the **10**........................ that we expect to happen. I will have to think about what **11**........................ to take about this and I will need to talk to your manager. I am now **12**........................ to work on this report myself this weekend.

Keiran

Grammar
should have

3 Find and correct five mistakes in sentences 1–8.

```
              have
1 We should/finished this last week.
              ∧
```

2 We probably should have extend the deadline.

3 We should haven't make William the team leader.

4 We should have heard from Helena by now.

5 We shouldn't have set such high standards.

6 We should have managed the project better.

7 She shouldn't have get such a bad grade.

8 They shouldn't had forced us to change the design.

4 Complete the conversations with the correct form of the verbs in the boxes and *should have* or *shouldn't have*.

> guess   lie   ~~tell~~

A: I'm sorry, I probably **1** *should have told* you earlier that I was applying for a new job.
B: Yes, you really **2**........................ and pretended to be sick when you went for the interview. As you looked fine the day before and the day after, I suppose I **3**........................ that you hadn't been ill.

> ask   do   ignore   realise   talk

A: So, the video showed a team leader ignoring a problem between two members of her team. What do you think she **4**........................ differently?
B: I think she probably **5**........................ them to come into her office to talk about it.
C: I disagree! I think first she **6**........................ to them independently, to find out more about the problem.
B: Well, we agree that she **7**........................ it.
C: Absolutely! She **8**........................ that that was only going to make the problem worse.

Vocabulary

Describing things

1 Choose the correct alternatives.

1 My new computer was such good *value/price* for money.
2 I had to call the helpline because I couldn't *set/last* up the printer.
3 The problem with electric cars is that the battery doesn't *last/set* long.
4 My old cooker still works really well, but it isn't very *feature/stylish*.
5 I think the camera is the best *feature/value* of my phone. It's amazing.
6 These lights turn on and off *reasonably/automatically* when you go in or out of the room.
7 This new washing machine has too many *tough/complicated* features.
8 My new laptop is pretty heavy, which isn't *ideal/stylish* for carrying around. Fortunately I only use it at home.

2 Complete the sentences using the words in the box.

> automatically   bargain   decent   designed   lasted   ~~leather~~
> reasonable   room

1 I'm vegetarian, so I would never buy shoes made of __*leather*__ .
2 I'm going to buy a more expensive laptop this time because my old one only _____ two years.
3 I paid £200 pounds less than the usual price for this table and I got two extra chairs for free. What a _____ !
4 Their car is nice, but there's only _____ for two people.
5 The computer comes with a _____ amount of memory.
6 This tent is really well _____ because you can pack it away into a small bag.
7 After 30 minutes, the device turns off _____ .
8 This phone screen is really _____ . I've dropped it three times, and it doesn't even have a scratch!

Grammar

Adjective word order

3 Rewrite the sentences so that the adjectives are in the correct order.

1 It's a big American red car.
  It's a big red American car.
2 I love your blue and orange Moroccan enormous carpet.
  _____
3 Have you seen Laila's big gold new ring?
  _____
4 Harriet's got a pair of grey fantastic leather boots.
  _____
5 It's a wooden tiny beautiful 1950s table.
  _____
6 Mr French always wears an old red disgusting jumper.
  _____
7 My neighbour has got a cute black and white little puppy.
  _____
8 I've just bought a lovely Italian big armchair for my apartment.
  _____

4 Complete the sentences using the adjectives in brackets in the correct order.

1 Mozzarella is a _____ _____ _____ cheese. (white, mild, Italian)
2 I saw a _____ _____ _____ chair in the market this morning. (leather, lovely, red)
3 My car is the _____ _____ _____ one near the exit. (yellow, small, dirty)
4 My sister only likes _____ _____ _____ jewellery. (silver, stylish, modern)
5 There's a _____ _____ _____ restaurant. (new, wonderul, Spanish)
6 It's a _____ _____ _____ building. (grey, strange, little)
7 They gave me a _____ _____ _____ horse to ride. (old, big, brown)
8 That's an _____ _____ _____ mask. (original, Mexican, clay)
9 I've seen a pair of _____ _____ _____ socks in a shop. (woollen, lovely, long)
10 I have this really _____ _____ _____ pair of trainers that I love. (comfortable, blue, old)

5 Complete the sentences with the adjectives in the box.

> ~~ancient~~   black and white   French   little
> ridiculous   stone

1 Petra is an enormous __*ancient*__ city in Jordan.
2 It's a really beautiful, big old French _____ farmhouse.
3 Rufus has bought a _____ huge new Italian SUV.
4 My friend has moved to a lovely _____ old English village.
5 My friend bought me an expensive mature _____ brandy for my birthday.
6 I've got a smelly 20-year-old _____ cat called Oscar.

Functional language
Offer and accept/decline

1 Choose the correct alternatives.

1 **A:** ¹*Would/Can* you like me to do that for you?
   B: ²*Please/Fine.*

2 **A:** Need any ³*help/hand*?
   B: It's OK. I can ⁴*manage/offer.*

3 **A:** ⁵*Let/Shall* I make you a cup of tea?
   B: That's very ⁶*kind/great* but I had one on the train.

4 **A:** Can I give you a ⁷*welcome/hand* with the cleaning?
   B: Would you ⁸*manage/mind*?

5 **A:** Feel ⁹*free/happy* to put the TV on.
   B: That would be ¹⁰ *OK/great*, thanks.

2 Complete the sentences with one word in each gap.

1 I'd be ___*happy*___ to pick you up from the airport, if you like.

2 Don't _____. I'm OK. The taxi will be here in a minute.

3 You're _____ to come shopping with me if you need anything.

4 I'm _____, thanks. I'm not thirsty.

5 Are you _____ you don't want me to write down the directions for you?

6 It's OK. There's no _____ for you to come with me to the bus stop.

7 Thanks for the _____ to make me lunch, but I'm fine.

8 _____ me carry those bags for you.

Listening

1 🔊 10.01 **Listen to the conversation and choose the correct summary.**

a The people agree which sofa Jen should buy.

b Jen decides which sofa to buy, though her friend doesn't agree with her choice.

c The people can't find a suitable sofa for Jen.

2 Listen again. Choose the correct option a, b or c.

1 Jen needs a sofa that …
   a isn't too small because her room is quite big.
   b isn't too small because she wants to sleep on it.
   c isn't too big because her room is quite small.

2 The Innsbruck sofa comes in …
   a three different colours.   b four different colours.
   c five different colours.

3 Jen likes the …
   a blue Innsbruck sofa.   b red Innsbruck sofa.
   c green Innsbruck sofa.

4 Jen can't buy the Innsbruck sofa because …
   a it isn't big enough.   b it isn't a sofa bed.   c it's too expensive.

5 The Yale sofa is …
   a cheaper than the Innsbruck sofa.
   b about the same price as the Innsbruck sofa.
   c more expensive than the Innsbruck sofa.

6 Jen doesn't want the Yale sofa because …
   a she doesn't like the colours.   b it isn't a sofa bed.
   c it isn't very stylish.

7 Jen thinks the Rockwell sofa is …
   a really attractive.   b really comfortable.
   c a really good bargain.

8 Jen wants to buy a … Rockwell sofa.
   a red   b orange   c pink

3 Listen again and complete the reviews.

👤 Rachel
★★★★★ **Great sofa!**
I recently bought the Rockwell sofa and I love it! I bought it in my favourite colour: bright ¹_____ . Amazing! It's modern and ²_____ .

👤 Andrew
★★★☆☆ **Could be better**
The Rockwell sofa is a great sofa, but not a good ³_____ . A bit disappointed.

👤 Fran
★★☆☆☆ **Too difficult to set up**
I would not recommend this sofa. It looks great now it's set up, but I had a lot of problems trying to ⁴_____ . The sofa came in ⁵_____ different pieces and the instructions were really ⁶_____ .

👤 Katie
★★☆☆☆ **Poor quality!** ☹
I bought this sofa in ⁷_____ . It looked great, but only lasted for ⁸_____ . Had to spend the same money again to buy a new sofa.

Reading

1 **Read the article. How does the writer feel about da Vinci's work?**

a negative

b extremely positive

c a mix of positive and negative

2 **Read the article again. Which of the following isn't mentioned?**

a when Leonardo da Vinci lived

b where he came from

c his famous paintings

3 **Complete the article with the words in the box.**

artist   explorers   military engineer   military leader   philosopher

A Leonardo da Vinci (1452–1519) was an incredible man who made a huge contribution to art and science during his lifetime. Most people become famous for one talent, but da Vinci had many talents. Some people think of him only as an ¹ _____ because he is famous for well-known paintings such as *The Last Supper* and *The Mona Lisa*. However, da Vinci often didn't complete the paintings he started. Only 15 paintings that we know were definitely painted by da Vinci exist today.

B Although da Vinci isn't known as a ² _____ , he was definitely a great thinker. Did you know that he was the first person to explain correctly why the sky is blue? He also discovered why we can see the outline of the moon when only a thin banana shape is showing. Da Vinci wrote down his ideas in his notebooks. He wanted to keep these ideas private, so he wrote with his left hand, writing from right to left. The only way someone can read da Vinci's notes is if they use a mirror.

C Da Vinci invented items that couldn't be made in the 15th century because the technology hadn't been developed. He drew designs for a flying machine, similar to an early helicopter. He also developed a piece of equipment that made it possible for ³ _____ to breathe underwater.

D In 1499, da Vinci travelled to Venice to work as a ⁴ _____ in the war against the Ottoman Empire. He planned to build something to control the flow of water into the Isonzo river valley. Another important idea was for divers to use underwater breathing equipment to swim under the enemy's ships and make holes in these ships so that they would sink.

E In 1502, da Vinci started to work for Cesare Borgia. Cesare Borgia was a very powerful man, and a ⁵ _____ in the army. Da Vinci's military inventions for Borgia included a machine gun, an army tank and a battleship. However, very few of da Vinci's inventions were successful. Some people believe that da Vinci deliberately designed these machines so that they wouldn't work! Although his job was to design military machines, he did not want these machines to be used to hurt others.

F Even though da Vinci didn't complete many of his projects, there are hundreds of examples of his extraordinary talent. Many of his ideas contributed to inventions which developed during the following centuries. Da Vinci once said that he would like to become famous so that he could be remembered for a long time. Five hundred years later, everyone knows the name Leonardo da Vinci, and we will remember him long into the future.

4 Read the text again and answer the questions.

According to the text …

1 How many of da Vinci's paintings exist today?

2 How did da Vinci keep his notes and ideas secret?

3 Why was da Vinci's helicopter never built when he was alive?

4 When did he travel to Venice?

5 Who gave da Vinci a job in 1502?

6 Why do some people think many of da Vinci's military machines did not work?

7 Why did da Vinci say he wanted to be famous?

5 Find words and phrases in the article to match definitions 1–8.

1 the part someone plays in making something happen
   .... (paragraph A)

2 a skill .... (paragraph A)

3 the shape of something .... (paragraph B)

4 items used for a particular purpose .... (paragraph C)

5 the movement of water .... (paragraph D)

6 to drop below the surface of the water .... (paragraph D)

7 new objects or ideas .... (paragraph E)

8 very unusual .... (paragraph F)

6 Read the text. What was David learning about when he heard about the natural disaster?

Thirteen-year-old American schoolboy David Cohen has shown that you have to be able to think differently if you want to have great ideas. At school, David was learning about worms and how they move. Then he heard about a natural disaster which destroyed many buildings in a nearby city. People were trapped under the buildings and it was difficult to rescue them. David wondered if it might be possible to design a robot worm that could go under the ground and rescue people. He designed this robot and won an award for it.

After this success, David started work on designing a different robot to solve another problem.

He thought about how mosquitos can carry dangerous diseases. He knew that mosquitos lay their eggs in water and the chemicals we use to kill mosquitos can pollute the water we drink. He thought it would be a good idea to stop the mosquitoes from growing up so that they couldn't fly and spread the diseases. David designed a robot to collect and then kill young mosquitos from the surface of the water before they are old enough to fly.

7 Read the text again, and decide which of the statements are true (T) or false (F).

1 David's first idea was inspired by something he studied. ....

2 He was involved in a natural disaster. ....

3 He created his first design because he wanted to help people. ....

4 His first robot was designed to travel beneath the earth. ....

5 People didn't recognise his achievement. ....

6 For his second invention, he studied another animal. ....

7 His second robot was designed to do the same thing as the first one. ....

8 His second invention may have a benefit for people's health ....

9 Both of his designs came from thinking about how to solve problems. ....

Writing

1 Read the essay. Does the writer focus mainly on the positive or negative aspects of Shakespeare's achievements?

2 Read the essay again and complete 1–3 with sentences a–c.

   a Shakespeare expanded the English language.
   b Shakespeare's influence on the English language can still be seen (and heard) today.
   c Shakespeare lived in the 16th century and became famous during his own lifetime.

3 Read the essay again. Are the sentences true (T) or false (F)?

   1 Shakespeare only wrote plays. ....
   2 The writer thinks that Shakespeare had a positive influence on the English language. ....
   3 Shakespeare was born in London. ....
   4 Shakespeare didn't have any children. ....
   5 Shakespeare joined The Lord Chamberlain's Men in 1592. ....
   6 Shakespeare's plays were performed for both a king and queen. ....
   7 Shakespeare invented 15,000 words. ....
   8 Academics claim that the English language would be poorer if Shakespeare had never written his plays. ....
   9 Both Agatha Christie and Alfred Hitchcock named some of their works after phrases from Shakespeare's plays. ....
   10 Many of Shakespeare's phrases are used in everyday English. ....

Choose an influential person. Describe who they are/ were, how they became famous and what they are famous for. Explain the positive and negative impacts of their achievements or actions.

William Shakespeare is considered one of the greatest English language writers and poets. He wrote at least 37 plays and a collection of poems, and his plays have been performed more often than the plays of any other writer. In this essay, I will explain who Shakespeare was, and why I think he was so influential. I will discuss his positive influence on the development of English as a language and how this is still relevant today.

1 .... He was born in 1564 in Stratford-upon-Avon, a small market town in England. He married Anne Hathaway in 1582 and they had three children together. He was lucky enough to have an education and he moved to London in the hope of developing a writing career. Shakespeare's first plays seem to have appeared around 1592. In 1594 he joined a theatre group called *The Lord Chamberlain's Men*. In 1599 he established the *Globe Theatre* so that the theatre group had somewhere in London to perform regularly. As well as entertaining the people of London, Shakespeare's plays were also performed at the royal court in front of Queen Elizabeth I and King James I.

2 .... Many of the English words and phrases that we use today first appeared in Shakespeare's plays. It is estimated that he used over 15,000 words in his plays, and academics believe that he invented many of them. They claim that Shakespeare's use of language was so rich that if he hadn't written his plays, the English language would not contain many of the words we use to say how we are feeling or how to talk about our experiences.

3 .... It can be seen in the titles of popular songs, books, plays and films, such as Agatha Christie's *The Mousetrap* and Alfred Hitchcock's *North by Northwest*, both of which have titles taken from Shakespeare plays. Furthermore, his influence can also be seen in thousands of English sayings, such as *to have a heart of gold*. Shakespeare has not only influenced what we read, but also the English that we speak.

4 Find and complete these sentences from the essay.

1 _____ entertaining the people of London, Shakespeare's plays were also performed at the royal court in front of Queen Elizabeth I and King James I.

2 _____, his influence can also be seen in thousands of English sayings, such as *to have a heart of gold*.

3 Shakespeare has _____ influenced what we read _____ the English that we speak.

5 Match the sentence halves.

1 We use *not only ... but also* and *as well as* _____

2 We use *Furthermore,* _____

3 We use the *-ing* form _____

a to add an idea connected to the previous sentence.

b to link two ideas in the same sentence.

c after *as well as*.

6 Complete the sentences using the words in bold to connect the ideas.

1 Shakespeare performed in front of Elizabeth I. He performed in front of James I.

not only ... but also

Shakespeare _____
James I.

2 He wrote tragedies. He wrote comedies and histories.

as well as

_____ , Shakespeare wrote comedies and histories.

3 Shakespeare wrote a lot of amazing plays. He wrote many beautiful poems.

furthermore

Shakespeare wrote a lot of amazing plays. _____
_____ .

7 Read the Focus box and then do Exercise 8.

Answering the essay question

Before you start writing an essay, read the instructions carefully and ask yourself these questions to make sure you write what you need to:

- What is the main topic of the essay?
- Is there a maximum number of things I should write about?
- Do I need to include any of the following?
  - [1] the background or history of something
  - [2] the reasons why something happened/is happening
  - [3] the effects of an event, product or process
  - [4] solutions to a problem
- Should I give my opinion about whether something is [5]positive or [6]negative?
- Is there a word limit?

In your answer, you need to make clear you are following the instructions by:

- explaining in your introduction how you are going to answer and in what order
- organising the essay into paragraphs
- using a sentence (usually at the start of a paragraph) to explain how the paragraph relates to the essay question.

8 Match sentences a–f from an essay about computers with points 1–6 in the Focus box.

a Constant working at a computer screen has had a negative effect on many people's eyesight. _____

b Children are being taught how to use computers in kindergarten because computer literacy has become the most important 21st century skill to have. _____

c However, computers have had a positive effect in terms of creating new industries, such as video games and social media. _____

d It is virtually impossible to switch off from work now that we have laptop computers and computers on our phones, and I think this has made our generation more stressed. _____

e The first mechanical computer was actually invented in 1822 by Charles Babbage, with help from Ada Lovelace. _1_

f It would be a good idea to have timers on our computers that makes them automatically switch off after a couple of hours and to stay off for at least half an hour. _____

Prepare

9a You're going to write an essay in response to the essay question in Exercise 1. Choose a person, living or dead, who you think has been very influential.

b Make notes using points 1–6 in the Focus box.

c Plan your essay.

- Paragraph 1 (introduction):
  _____
  _____

- Paragraph 2:
  _____
  _____

- Paragraph 3:
  _____
  _____

- Paragraph 4 (conclusion):
  _____

Write

10 Write your essay using your notes from Exercise 9 and the ideas in the Focus box to help you.

UNIT 1 Recording 1

P = Presenter   O = Onni

P: Good evening and welcome to the programme. I'm Deborah Kapoor and you're listening to *Nights on Earth*, the programme that asks people, 'What do you do at night?' This evening, my guest is Onni, who comes from Finland. Welcome to the programme, Onni.

O: Thanks, Deborah.

P: So, Onni, please tell us about nights in Finland.

O: Well, Finland is quite extraordinary because we have two different kinds of nights: white nights and polar nights.

P: Really? And what's the difference between these two kinds of nights, umm … polar and … ?

O: Polar and white nights. Well, in Finland, for two months in the winter, from the end of November to the end of January, the sun doesn't rise.

P: Not at all?

O: No, not at all.

P: So, it's nighttime for two whole months?

O: Yes. It's completely dark – we call this the polar night.

UNIT 1 Recording 2

P = Presenter   O = Onni

P: So, do people just sleep for two months?

O: Ha! Well, yes, people do sleep a lot, but we do still have to go to work and school, and do all the usual things, like shopping …

P: It must be quite difficult if there's no daylight.

O: Yes, and some people get very sad in the winter months in Finland, but there are things you can do to help you during the polar nights.

P: Can you give us an example?

O: Well, we buy special lamps for our houses. These are really powerful and they make your brain believe that it's daytime.

P: Oh, that's clever. What else do you do?

O: Well, you have to keep busy, so many of us see this as a time to take up a new hobby, see friends, paint our homes, learn a new language … that sort of thing.

P: I see – but it still must be very difficult.

O: Yes, I think it can be, especially for visitors who aren't used to it. However, we know that we just have to wait a few months and then we will have the white nights.

P: Oh yes, the white nights. So, are they the summer nights?

O: Yes.

P: And how are these different to the polar nights?

O: Well, for two months in the summer, July and August, the sun never sets.

P: Ah! So it's always daytime?

O: Yes, it never gets completely dark.

P: How do you know when to sleep?

O: To be honest, we sleep very little during those months. Maybe for an hour or two at a time. It's party or holiday season. There are lots of all-night festivals and parties, of course, but we also just do everything we would usually do in the daytime. We might go swimming in the lake, go hiking, canoeing, fishing, golf – whatever it is we like to do outdoors.

P: And you might go fishing at two in the morning?

O: Definitely.

P: Fascinating. It's almost like you have two different lives – a winter life and a summer life.

O: Yes, I suppose it is.

P: Well, thanks very much, Onni, for coming on to the programme today …

UNIT 2 Recording 1

C = Camilla   G = George

C: Hello, everyone. My name is Camilla Lopez and I'm the Staff Manager here. This induction meeting is going to be fairly informal – I just want to go through some information with you about company policies. You'll have a chance to ask any questions at the end.

Let's start with some basic health and safety rules. We regularly have fire drills so that we know what to do in case of fire. When you hear the fire alarm, please don't use the lifts. Walk down the stairs and meet in the car park at the back of the building. Each department meets in a special place – please look on this map to find exactly where you need to go.

We run first aid courses from time to time, so please let me know if this is something you might be interested in. We must have at least two people in each department who have taken the course, so we are keen to get as many people as possible to do it.

As an employee of this company, you are now also a member of the union. You can contact them or speak to your union representative if you need any advice or help. All contact details are on the company website.

There's a strict policy on clothes. Please make sure that you always wear formal clothes. I know that most companies in this area tend to let their employees wear casual dress on Fridays, but I'm afraid that we're not one of them. We're constantly in contact with customers, so we need to look formal at all times.

As a rule, the company has fairly flexible working hours, for example, if you need to change shifts or take some time off. Please try to talk to your manager in advance though. Some people have a habit of asking for time off the day before and then we might not be able to be so flexible.

I think that's about it. Does anyone have any questions … ? Yes?

G: Hi, Camilla. My name is George and I've just joined the computing department. Can I ask what the company policy is on break times?

C: Yes, of course. You get one hour for lunch every day.

G: And is the time of the lunch break flexible?

C: You need to talk to your manager about that. I'm sure they will try to be flexible if you need to take your break at a certain time.

G: That's great, thank you.

C: Any other questions … ? No? OK, well, I won't keep you any longer. If you do think of anything else you'd like to ask, then feel free to email me or come and see me on the fourth floor. My door is always open!

UNIT 3   Recording 1

Z = Zara   P = Patrick

P: So, have you got any holiday plans for this year?

Z: Yes, actually, I'm thinking of going to Africa.

P: Oh, OK. Have you been there before?

Z: Yeah, I've been to Morocco four times and I went to Egypt last year, but I've never been to South Africa. I know that it's supposed to be amazing. You've travelled a lot around there, haven't you?

P: Yes, I have. I spent three months in South Africa when I was a student. I worked on a nature reserve.

Z: Oh, I'd love to visit a nature reserve.

P: Yeah, it was in a beautiful spot and the landscape was incredible.

Z: I'd really like to go there sometime. What else is there to do in South Africa?

P: There are lots of interesting things to see. The coast is beautiful, and Cape Town and Johannesburg are really cool cities. Have you ever visited a gold mine?

Z: No, I haven't!

P: You can do a guided tour of one of the oldest mines in the country. The Kromdraai Gold Mine is only a 40-minute drive north of Johannesburg. Oh, and you could also visit one of the oldest buildings in South Africa – the Castle of Good Hope. It was built in the 17th century by Dutch people. That's in Cape Town.

Z: So, is it better to stay in Johannesburg or in Cape Town?

P: Well, the cities aren't too far apart, so you can spend some time in both places. It takes about two hours to travel between them by plane.

Z: Oh, OK. I'm going to do some more research this weekend and then I think I'll book my trip! What about you? Have you and Jess decided where you're going to go this year?

P: No, I've got no idea! We've got three weeks free in August. Have you got any suggestions?

Z: Have you ever been to Indonesia?

P: No, I haven't. I know that it's supposed to be beautiful.

Z: Yes, it's stunning. I went there three years ago and I had an amazing time.

P: What can you do there?

Z: Have you ever been surfing?

P: Yes, I have! I love it!

Z: Then you'll love Indonesia – it's got some of the most amazing surf beaches in the world. I think the best island to visit for surfing is Bali.

P: Jess likes sightseeing though. She'll get bored if we're on the beach all day. Are there some interesting sites to visit?

Z: Absolutely! Have you ever been to an ancient temple?

P: No, we haven't, but we'd love to!

Z: There are lots of beautiful temples in great spots along the coast. Some of them are hundreds of years old. I don't think Jess will be bored!

P: The food is supposed to be delicious, isn't it?

Z: Oh yes, I love it. It's full of interesting spices and flavours. My favourite Indonesian food is chicken satay – it's so good! You have to try it!

P: OK, well, it sounds amazing. I'll talk to Jess about it tonight.

Z: We've just planned our next holidays for each other!

P: I know, very helpful!

UNIT 4   Recording 1

J = Jude   K = Kim

J: So, did you hear about the robbery at the local shop last week?

K: I know! It's terrible. Did I tell you what happened to my friend last year?

J: No. What happened?

K: I was walking down the high street with my friend, Claire. All of a sudden, a motorbike with two people on it came out of nowhere. It was going very fast. We jumped out of the way, but the person on the back of the bike pulled Claire's bag off her shoulder. It had her laptop in it. She tried to hold on to it but they were going too fast and she couldn't. She fell into the street.

J: Was she hurt?

K: Not badly, but she was very shocked.

J: So her laptop was stolen?

K: Yeah.

J: I bet she was really angry.

K: Yes, she was. It was awful. We had to report it to the police.

J: Did she get her laptop back?

K: No. And she'd just finished an essay for college on it. She was so upset. What about you? Have you ever witnessed a crime?

J: No, but I *have* been the victim of one.

K: Have you? I didn't know that.

J: I don't really talk about it much. To be honest, I feel a bit embarrassed by it.

K: Really? Why?

J: Well, I suppose it was partly my fault.

K: How?

J: I wasn't really being careful enough.

K: Where were you?

J: I was in Paris, near the Eiffel Tower. I think I probably looked like a tourist.

K: So, what happened?

J: I stopped to have a coffee at an outside café and I put my backpack on the chair opposite me. It was a silly thing to do, really. I usually keep it on my back. Suddenly this girl who was walking past spilt a bit of her drink on my leg. I turned around to speak to her. She looked really embarrassed and kept apologising. I felt sorry for her, so I told her not to worry as no one had been hurt. When I looked around again, my backpack had gone.

K: Oh no! So she was a thief?

J: Yes, I think she was probably working as part of a gang. While she was talking to me someone else took my backpack.

K: Oh! I bet that really ruined your holiday.

J: Yes, it did a bit.

K: Was your passport in your backpack?

J: Luckily, it wasn't, but I did lose quite a lot of money, as well as some souvenirs I'd bought for my family.

K: That's awful! Did you report it to the police?

J: No, I didn't, actually. I just wanted to forget about it.

P = Presenter   A = Anna

P: Good morning and welcome to the programme. I'm Greg Heller and you're listening to *In my town*, the programme that keeps you up to date with what's happening locally. Today, we have restaurant owner, Anna Marchant with us. Hello, Anna.

A: Hello, Greg.

P: Thanks for being here.

A: My pleasure.

P: Now, Anna, you already own a café and a small restaurant, so you're a very busy lady.

A: Yes, I am.

P: And yet, you've got another project going on at the moment?

A: That's right – I have. I'm in the process of opening a new restaurant.

P: Fantastic! But why? Why open a third place?

A: Well, I love food, of course and, honestly, I think I get bored very easily. One evening, I was chatting with a chef friend, and we were talking about our favourite restaurants and what makes a restaurant great, and we realised we'd created an idea for a new restaurant of our own.

P: And so you decided to go ahead and make it happen.

A: Yes. Why not?

P: I think a lot of listeners, and myself included, would say that's a great idea, but there's no way I could set up and run **one** restaurant, let alone three!

A: Maybe. Maybe we're both just a little bit crazy.

P: I don't think that's true. So, tell us, where's it going to be?

A: In James Street, right in the centre of the old town.

P: Fabulous! And what's it going to be called?

A: It's going to be called *Green shoots*.

P: *Green shoots*. Why have you chosen that name?

A: Because the food I'm going to serve will all be foraged locally.

P: Foraged?

A: Yes. Foraging is when you find and collect food that is growing naturally, so for example, I might pick berries from bushes by the side of the road, or find mushrooms in the woods.

P: Wow! That sounds amazing.

A: Thanks. I'm passionate about serving fresh, local, seasonal food.

P: But you won't be able to forage for everything on the menu presumably?

A: Sadly, no, but I'll buy the rest of the food from local farms.

P: And how long have you been planning and working on the new restaurant?

A: Planning, for about three years. The actual building work started ten months ago.

P: And when will the restaurant open?

A: Well, it was meant to open in July, but unfortunately we've had some building problems. It's in a really old 15th century building and the builders realised about two months ago that the ceiling wasn't safe.

P: Oh no!

A: Yes, it's a shame, because it means the building work has cost about £20,000 more than we'd expected it to. But, the building has to be safe.

P: Yes, of course.

A: So now we're having a launch party on the 23rd August. And of course, you're invited. It'll start at seven in the evening.

P: I can't wait! Well, Anna, I wish you every success with *Green shoots*.

A: Thanks, Greg.

N = Nina   H = Hassan

N: I've just finished watching the last episode of *This Beautiful World*.

H: Oh yes, I saw that, too. The ending was great, wasn't it? I can't believe they killed off the main character in the last scene, though. It means that they can't do another series now.

N: I know! I was nearly in tears when Martin Harris died. It was so sad and so well acted. I never wanted it to end. I don't know what I'm going to do with myself now. I need another series to watch. Have you got any recommendations?

H: I'm watching that talent show, *True or Terrible*, at the moment.

N: Hmmm, I'm not sure about that. Those sorts of programmes generally just make me want to switch over.

H: I don't usually like them either, but this one is hilarious. It's made in Australia, and some of the people in the show are useless! Last night, this singer was voted off because she just couldn't sing and she forgot her words, too. It was so embarrassing, but it really made me laugh!

N: No, I don't like the sound of that. I just find talent shows a bit dull. Also, I feel sorry for the people who get voted off. I much prefer to watch interesting dramas. I like TV programmes that are well written with characters that you can believe in.

H: Oh, I saw a film last week that you might like.

N: Oh yes?

H: It was a drama about two brothers who live in Los Angeles. They run a restaurant together, but then one of them gets married and they start having all sorts of problems. The dialogue was excellent, and the ending was so tense. I was really stressed watching it!. The actors were great, too. One of the brothers was played by Derek Sams.

N: Oh, yes, I like him. What's the film called?

H: *The Sound Garden*. I watched it at the cinema last week. But I don't think it's going to be on for much longer. Try to go this weekend if you want to see it. I also saw that new science fiction film, *The Day of Arrival*.

N: Oh yeah, I've heard of that. Any good?

H: It was OK. It was a typical Hollywood blockbuster. The special effects were good, but there wasn't much of a story and the acting was terrible. I wouldn't waste your money on that.

N: To be honest, I hardly ever go to the cinema anymore. It's just so expensive.

H: Yeah, I know what you mean.

N: I pay for a streaming service every month and there are hundreds and hundreds of films to watch on there. I'm never going to run out of things to watch!

H: Yes, but you can't beat that cinema experience, when the lights go off and all you can see is that huge screen. I love to lose myself in a film.

N: Well, I'd rather watch films in my bed on my laptop! The seats in the cinema aren't as warm and comfortable as my bed!

H: Ha! Yes, good point!

I = Isla   S = Stefan

I: Hi, Stefan. Lovely to see you. I've just been looking at your photos of China that you posted. They're amazing! When did you get back?

S: Hi, Isla. Good to see you, too. I got back on Saturday.

I: I loved your pictures of the water town.

S: You mean Wuzhen? Yeah, it was totally amazing! It's just south of the Yangtze River and it's over 7,000 years old. You can only get around the town by boat, so you have to take a water taxi to get to your hotel.

I: It sounds like Venice in Italy.

S: Yes, very similar, though not nearly as big.

I: Have you been to Venice then?

S: Yes, I have, actually. I went two years ago. It's incredible. Did you know that Venice is built on 118 separate islands and that people have lived there since Roman times? That makes it around 1,600 years old!

I: No, I didn't know that.

S: You can't drive around Venice, so everyone travels by boat. They have ambulance boats, police boats, boats for rubbish, and lots of boats for other things, too. And of course the famous vaporetti, which is the water taxi.

I: I thought the gondola was the water taxi.

S: No, not anymore. Gondolas are just for tourists.

I: Oh, I see. So, have you been to any other water cities, then?

S: Well, yes, I have, in fact, because I find water cities really interesting. I've been to Mexicaltitán in Mexico. It's called 'the Venice of Mexico'.

I: Wow! I've never heard of it.

S: It's built on a man-made island, which is only 400 metres in diameter. In the dry season, it's just a normal island, but in the wet season, the island floods and you can only travel around it by canoe.

I: And people live there?

S: Yep! Over 800 people live there.

I: Are there any other water towns around the world?

S: Yes. I haven't visited them all yet, but I plan to.

I: Really? Where?

S: I'd really like to go to Ganvie in Benin.

I: Is that in Asia?

S: No, it's in Africa. It's a village on a lake.

I: Do you mean on an island in a lake?

S: No, it's actually built over Lake Nokoue, so all the houses are built on stilts and stick up out of the water.

I: So, I imagine you can't walk around it at all.

S: No. The people who live there travel around in canoes called *pirogues*.

I: Do lots of people live there?

S: Well, there are about 3,000 buildings and between 20 and 30 thousand people, I think.

I: Wow! I never knew so many people lived on the water.

S: I know. It's amazing, isn't it? I think I might only travel to water towns and cities from now on.

I: Well, I might just come with you on one of your trips.

P = Presenter   M = Maria

P: Hello, and welcome to *Book Hour* on Radio Live. Joining me in the studio today is Maria Costa, author of over 20 books and winner of several book prizes. Hello, Maria, and thank you for coming in today.

M: It's a pleasure. Thank you for inviting me.

P: So, tell us first a bit about your early life. Where were you born?

M: I was born in Italy in 1952, in a small town near Sicily. I had a very happy childhood. My mother was English, my father was Spanish and I grew up in Italy, so we spoke all three languages in my house! I think that's where my love of words and language comes from. Also, my parents were both teachers, so I remember there were always a lot of books lying around the house. I grew up surrounded by them. When I was at school, I loved writing, and I ended up studying English Literature at college in the US.

P: And how old were you when you wrote your first book?

M: I wrote it when I was 22! I took a year off after I graduated. I always knew that I wanted to write books, but I didn't know if I could do it as a job. So, I gave myself a year to see if I could write a good book and get it published. That was when I wrote *Ivy's Beach*.

P: And was it published immediately?

M: No, it wasn't. I sent it to about 20 publishing companies and they all said no. They were too frightened to publish a book by a new author. But I kept trying until I found somebody who said yes! And I'm still with the same publisher today. I'm so grateful that they took a chance on me.

P: So, what happened after your first book was published?

M: I moved back to Italy for a while, and that's where I met my first husband, Marco. After we announced our engagement, we moved to the UK. We got married in 1979.

P: You were writing a lot during your twenties, weren't you?

M: Yes, I was. I had four books published. I couldn't stop writing! I got pregnant the year after I got married and gave birth to my son, Paul. Then my daughter, Alex, was born two years later. My early thirties were busy years with two young children, so I didn't have very much time to write.

P: But you came back to writing again, didn't you? I think that the books you wrote in your late thirties were more serious than your early novels.

M: Yes, you're right. I think I grew up a lot during that period. My father died four years after my daughter was born. Then my husband and I separated and we got divorced a couple of years later. Suddenly, I was alone with two kids. I had to earn money to look after them, so I started writing again.

P: Which book did you win your first prize for?

M: That was *Orange Marmalade*, which I wrote in 1990. I was so happy to win that prize and it was a real turning point in my life. Not only was my work going well, but I was happy in a new relationship, and my kids were enjoying life at school. That was when I realised that everything was going to be OK.

P: Thanks, Maria. We need to take a break now for the news but we'll be straight back with more questions.

P = Presenter   GR = Dr Gavi Ramireshi

P: Hello, and welcome to this week's podcast. Experience shows that to be a successful sports star you have to train hard from an early age, but recently many child and sports psychologists have argued that this is wrong. Here to explain further is child sports psychologist, Dr Gavi Ramiresh. Welcome, Dr Ramiresh.

GR: Thank you for inviting me.

P: So, in your recent article *Free to play* you say that it's possible to produce sporting stars without training very young children in the sport. Is that correct?

GR: Absolutely. Research shows that training children in one sport from a young age …

P: Sorry to interrupt, but when you say from a young age, what age are you thinking of?

GR: Well, we see some children as young as three or four being trained in only one sport.

P: Thank you. Please do go on.

GR: Yes, so as I was saying, research shows that training children in one sport from a young age isn't good for their physical development.

P: Could you explain what you mean?

GR: Yes. Young children need to develop their movement skills and their coordination. They do this by moving in all kinds of ways and by using lots of different play and sporting equipment. The best way to make sure they develop properly is to involve them in free play.

P: What do you mean by 'free play'?

GR: Free play is play without rules or being told how to play, unlike what happens when they are taught only one sport.

P: So, are you saying that children should not be taught any 'proper' sports until they are much older?

GR: No, I'm saying that the majority of their time should not involve *only* being taught one sport, as it will not teach them all the skills they need to learn.

P: OK, but there are a lot of children who are very talented at a particular sport. Are you suggesting that we shouldn't let them play that sport?

GR: No, I think if a child shows talent and, more importantly, interest, in any one sport, then they should be encouraged to play that sport, but only focus on a particular sport when they are much older.

P: So, at what age would you say they can start to focus on a particular sport?

GR: When they become teenagers.

P: But many sports coaches would say that that's too late, and that talented sports stars need to start training much earlier.

GR: I would disagree. No one should be expected to know what they want to do with their lives when they are children. In general, a child who is pushed too hard towards a sporting career can become a sporting failure by the time they are in their early twenties.

P: When you look at the lives of many of our sporting successes, they started training at a young age. Doesn't that suggest you're wrong?

GR: Perhaps, but there are also many who fail due to being pushed too hard when they were young. Studies have shown that these young adults can experience mental health issues. This is because they have grown up only

ever being told what they've done wrong rather than what they've done right.

P: Very interesting. Thanks to my guest, Dr Gavi Ramiresh, and I hope you enjoyed this week's podcast …

M = Meera   J = Jen

M: Hi, Jen. What are you doing?

J: Hi, Meera, I'm trying to choose a new sofa. I'm looking through all these brochures but there are just too many to choose from.

M: Would you like me to give you a hand?

J: Ah, would you mind?

M: Not at all. What sort of sofa do you want?

J: Well, it can't be too big because my room is tiny, but I do need it to be a sofa bed so that friends can come and stay.

M: OK, so a small sofa bed. What about this one, the Innsbruck sofa? It's for two people and comes in five different colours.

J: Ooh – yes, I like that. The blue one is lovely. Very stylish. Oh no! Look at the price though. I can't afford that.

M: Hmmm, what about the Yale design then? It's about the same size, but quite a bit cheaper.

J: Yes, but it's not a sofa bed.

M: Oh yes, you're right. The Yale sofa is no good then.

J: Ooh! What's that one? That's really stylish.

M: Yes, and it's quite reasonably priced.

J: What's it called?

M: Er, the Rockwell sofa. It comes in bright red, neon orange or hot pink!

J: Gosh, I love the hot pink one. It would look perfect in my room.

M: Let's find an online review. It's always helpful to read what people who have bought something actually think of it.

J: Good idea. Though I'm not sure you can trust all of those reviews. I often find that one person loves something and the next person hates it.

M: Maybe, but let's just see.

J: OK.

M: OK, so this person, Rachel, loves her Rockwell sofa. It says she bought the bright red one and thinks it's really modern and also really comfortable.

J: Excellent – I'm going to buy one now.

M: Wait a minute, though. This person, Andrew, says that it looks great, and although it's comfortable as a sofa, it's not great as a bed.

J: Well, I suppose friends don't come to stay too often.

M: Oh, and Fran says she had real problems trying to put it together. She says it comes in eight different pieces and the instructions are really confusing.

J: I'm sure I can get my brother to set it up. He's fantastic at that sort of thing. I really, really like this sofa. It's so stylish!

M: Well, Katie says her orange one didn't last. She had to buy another sofa after only two years. Although it's a good price, it's not very good value for money if it's going to fall apart that quickly.

J: I don't care. I'm buying it in hot pink right now.

ANSWER KEY

UNIT 1

1A

1
1 vegetarian 2 service 3 allergic 4 terrace
5 spicy 6 delicious 7 packed 8 set menu

2
1 packed 2 set menu 3 vegetarian
4 delicious 5 spicy 6 terrace 7 heaters
8 value

3
1 I'm allergic to cheese.
2 My sister is a vegetarian.
3 Shall I book in advance for dinner on Saturday night?
4 We had fantastic service last night./
  The service was fantastic last night.
5 We waited ages for a table.
6 The set menu costs/is £15.
7 They have definitely put up the prices.
8 I think the place would suit everyone.

4
1 order 2 place 3 fancy 4 top 5 value
6 plenty

5
1 d 2 a 3 e 4 b 5 f 6 c

6
1 that/which 2 who 3 in 4 to 5 to
6 next 7 where 8 to

1B

1
1 b 2 a 3 a 4 c 5 c 6 a 7 c 8 b

2
1 landlord 2 tidy 3 knock down 4 storage
5 tiny 6 freezing 7 cost 8 do

3
1 The city is a lot more exciting than the village.
2 This place is in slightly better condition than my last apartment.
3 Chelsea is far more lively than other neighbourhoods.
4 I'd like to live somewhere a bit cheaper than here.
5 The bedroom is even tinier than the living room.
6 This apartment isn't nearly as expensive as my brother's.

4
1 slightly 2 a lot 3 much 4 quite 5 even
6 far

5
1 My parents' house is much **bigger** than mine.
2 correct
3 My neighbourhood is **a bit** quieter than some areas.
4 This apartment isn't nearly **large** enough for all of us.
5 correct
6 Kerry's apartment is much **tidier** than Martin's.
7 The bedroom at the back of the house isn't quite as **big** as the bedroom at the front.
8 correct

1C

1
1 in 2 out 3 till 4 up 5 in 6 on 7 to
8 up

2
1 talking 2 queue 3 throwing 4 celebrate
5 episode 6 worth 7 missed 8 fortune
9 home 10 play

3
1 b 2 b 3 a 4 b 5 b 6 a 7 c 8 b

4
1 Last night I went to watch a ballet, which was brilliant.
2 I threw a party for Rachel, whose birthday is next week.
3 Samira went to the opera in Paris, where she saw Tosca.
4 I queued behind a lot of people, most of whom already had tickets.
5 I stayed up late last night, which is why I was tired this morning./I stayed up late last night, which meant I was tired this morning.
6 John studied in Madrid, where he met his girlfriend.
7 We're going to miss the last metro, which means we'll have to catch a taxi.
8 Dan and I went to a café before the show, which didn't start until three o'clock.

1D

1
1 e 2 f 3 a 4 d 5 b 6 g 7 h 8 c

2
1 b 2 f 3 a 4 g 5 d 6 e 7 h 8 c

Listening

1
c

2
1 Nights on Earth 2 two 3 polar

3
1 F *People do sleep a lot.*
2 F *... we still have to work and go to school.*
3 F *Some people get very sad in the winter months in Finland.*
4 T *These are really powerful and they make your brain believe it is daytime.*
5 T *... you have to keep busy*
6 F *... especially for visitors who aren't used to it*
7 T *... for two months in the summer, July and August, the sun never sets.*
8 F *We might go swimming in the lake, go hiking, canoeing, fishing ...*

4
1 rise 2 two 3 November 4 January
5 summer 6 set 7 two 8 night

Reading

1
b

2
1 c 2 a 3 b

3
1 California, USA 2 three 3 furniture
4 Tokyo, Japan 5 three 6 height
7 ancient 8 Warsaw, Poland 9 artist
10 92 cm 11 two

4
1 Because they have clear ideas about their dream homes.
2 He's a former world skateboarding champion.
3 Everywhere: up the walls, on the ceiling and on the furniture.
4 All energy in the house comes from the sun and the wind.
5 Because it has got huge windows instead of walls.
6 From an ancient Japanese belief that trees are very important.
7 Because he chose to build it in a tiny space between two buildings.
8 He used glass brick walls.

5
1 traditional 2 cosy 3 eco-friendly
4 bright 5 stylish 6 original 7 ancient
8 smooth

6
The Skateboard House

7
1 a 2 a 3 b 4 a 5 c 6 c 7 a

Writing

1
1 informal 2 formal 3 formal 4 formal
5 informal 6 informal 7 formal 8 formal

2
1 Formal: Tina is confirming a reservation of six bedrooms.
2 Informal: She's confirming details of the weekend to her friends and family.

3
1 F *They're celebrating the 25th anniversary.*
2 T
3 T
4 F *She asks the hotel to give her rooms with a view of the garden.*
5 F *She asks the hotel to make special arrangements for her grandmother.*
6 T
7 T
8 F *She asks friends to send her photographs for a special album she's making.*

4
1 Email 2 2 Email 1 3 Email 1 4 Email 2
5 Email 2 6 Email 1

5
Formal requests:
I was wondering if we could ...
I would be most grateful if you could ...
Do you think you could possibly ... ?
Would you mind ... ?
Would it be possible to ... ?
Informal requests:
Please email me back ...
Can you let me know mind if ... ?
Could you send them over to me ... ?

6
1 grateful 2 possible 3 wondering 4 mind
5 think 6 Could 7 you 8 Please

7
1 F: Dear Sir/Madam I: Hi everyone
2 F: I am writing to confirm ...
   I: Just a quick email to say ...
3 F: none I: We're/I've/I'm/I'll/it's
4 F: Best regards I: Cheers

8 and **9**
Students' own answers

UNIT 2

2A

1
1 out 2 on 3 at 4 of 5 at 6 over
7 to 8 of

2
1 d 2 h 3 a 4 b 5 f 6 c 7 e 8 g

3
1 develop 2 training 3 improve 4 skilled
5 expert 6 interested 7 challenge 8 keen

4
1 I **train** at the sports centre every Tuesday and Thursday.
2 correct
3 Ashanti **is downloading** an app at the moment.
4 **Do you understand** what I mean?

5 The word 'expert' **means** someone who is good at something.
6 correct
7 Yin and Michael **belong** to a golf club.
8 correct

5
1 are, doing 2 hate 3 'm having
4 'm doing 5 'm going 6 are doing 7 feel
8 don't think 9 isn't 10 Do, want

2B

1
1 flexible 2 time 3 strict 4 formal
5 casual 6 health 7 fire 8 first

2
1 b 2 c 3 b 4 c 5 a 6 c 7 b 8 a

3
1 Most people tend to get to the office by 9 a.m.
2 We regularly offer first aid courses to staff.
3 This computer has a habit of crashing.
4 We have union meetings from time to time.
5 As a rule, there's a strict policy on recycling.
6 Philippe doesn't tend to take time off in January.
7 Employees normally wear casual clothes on Fridays.
8 We don't tend to work after 6 p.m.

4
1 a 2 a 3 b 4 a 5 a 6 b 7 b 8 a

2C

1
1 c 2 b 3 b 4 b 5 c 6 a 7 a 8 a

2
1 I **broke** my arm when we were on holiday in Greece in 2014.
2 correct
3 I **used to live/lived** in Spain when I was a child.
4 Julia never **used to** play the piano.
5 correct
6 One time, I **saw** a jellyfish in the sea!
7 correct
8 Did you **use to** walk to school when you were a child?

3
1 control 2 force 3 watch 4 arrangements
5 let 6 authority 7 manners 8 trouble

4
1 h 2 f 3 g 4 b 5 e 6 c 7 a 8 d

5
1 b 2 c 3 f 4 g 5 h 6 e 7 d 8 a

2D

1
1 Listen 2 got 3 actually 4 to leave
5 been 6 off 7 up 8 run

2
1 Sorry to interrupt, but I need to get going.
2 I've got a class at 6.30.
3 My train is about to leave.
4 It was great to catch up.
5 Sorry to rush off like this.
6 Enjoy the rest of your evening!
7 See you soon.

Listening

1
c and d

2
1 It's an induction meeting to give new employees information about company policies.
2 The meeting is fairly informal.
3 Camilla is the Staff Manager.
4 George has just joined the computing department.
5 It's on the fourth floor.

3
1 safety 2 fire 3 car park 4 department
5 First aid 6 Union 7 Strict 8 formal
9 shifts 10 Break

Reading

1
c

2
a 3 **b** 2 **c** 1 **d** 4 **e** 5

3
1 article 2 true 3 report 4 quickly
5 mustn't be too big 6 quickly

4
1 b 2 b 3 a 4 c 5 a 6 a 7 b 8 c

5
1 Repeat an action again and again until you can do it.
2 The more you practise, the more highly skilled you will become at any activity.
3 2008
4 They were asked to learn how to control a computer with a new type of mouse.
5 That the people who practised in a slightly different way the second time did twice as well as the people who practised in exactly the same way the second time.
6 They help us understand how the brain remembers information and learns new things.
7 He's the scientist who led the research.
8 It could help people who have hurt their backs or their brains and who have to learn to walk or talk again.

6
1 expert 2 prove 3 session 4 research
5 improvement 6 leisure 7 technique
8 recover

Writing

1
1 informal 2 friend 3 news

2
1 F *Long time, no see.*
2 F *We've just come back from holiday. We spent two weeks in Croatia*
3 T *I was happy because I managed to finish three whole books!*
4 F *Jaber was happy because he got to go running every day.*
5 F *... the kids were happy because they enjoyed the water sports, though I think they got a bit bored by the end.*
6 T *Let's get a date in the diary for lunch or dinner soon.*
7 F *Marta's company has won an award.*
8 T *Dominic is well and has just had a promotion at work.*
9 F *The kids are fine, but I can never get Tom off his phone!*
10 F *We're about to be taken over by Kliemens and Sons.*
11 T *I think that some people will be made redundant.*
12 T *I might see if there are any jobs at Martins Harris because I heard that they're expanding.*

4
1 Long time, no see!
2 The landscape was stunning!
3 We went for long walks and ate lots of delicious food.
   He woke up every morning at 6 a.m., so he could go for a run along the beach before breakfast! I'd definitely like to go back one day, but maybe not with the kids.
   Also, the kids were happy because they enjoyed the water sports, though I think they got a bit bored by the end.
   It was a good holiday because there was something for everyone.
4 We spent two weeks in Croatia – it was so relaxing!
5 How are things with you?
   Have you been away yet this summer?
6 Can you believe that?
   Who knows?

5
1 c 2 b 3 b 4 a 5 c 6 b 7 a 8 b

6
1 g 2 d 3 f 4 h 5 a 6 b 7 c 8 e

7
1 Rh 2 R 3 Rh 4 Rh 5 R 6 R 7 Rh
8 Rh

8–10
Students' own answers

UNIT 3

3A

1
1 f 2 c 3 a 4 g 5 b 6 e 7 h 8 d

2
1 tour 2 medieval 3 restored 4 steep
5 view 6 climb 7 nature reserve 8 cliff

3
1 A: Have you ever been to France?
   B: Yes, I've been four times.
2 A: Have you ever been to the ancient temple?
   B: No, I haven't, but I'd love to go sometime.
3 A: Have you visited the hot springs?
   B: No, but I'm thinking of going tomorrow.
4 A: Have you looked around the coal mine?
   B: No, but it's supposed to be very interesting.
5 A: Have you climbed that steep mountain yet?
   B: No, but I'm going to do it tomorrow.

4
A: **Have you ever been** to Italy?
B: Yeah, **I've** been three times.
A: Oh, OK. Have you ever **visited** Rome?
B: Yeah, I spent three weeks there last August. I **did** a tour around the city while I was there. **It was** amazing there.
A: Did you go to Granada last summer?
B: No, but it's **supposed** to be wonderful. **I'd** love to go sometime.
A: I'm thinking **of** going next year. I'm going to book it this weekend!

3B

1
1 research 2 causes 3 cells 4 invested
5 cure 6 explored 7 risk 8 genes

2
1 c 2 c 3 a 4 b 5 c 6 a

3
1 identifying genes 2 Solar power
3 global birth rate 4 earthquake
5 increased dramatically 6 fallen steadily
7 predict

4
1 a has been studying b has read
2 a have been doing b has won
3 a has predicted b has been researching
4 a has been travelling b has visited

5
1 have read/'ve read
2 have been reading/'ve been reading
3 have been/'ve been
4 have been looking
5 have agreed
6 have known/'ve known
7 has he been playing
8 has the author written
9 have/'ve been working
10 have scientists discovered

3C

1
1 a 2 c 3 c 4 a 5 b 6 b

2
1 are required to/'re required to
2 are allowed to/'re allowed to
3 are supposed to/'re supposed to

4 aren't required to
5 aren't supposed to
6 aren't allowed to

3
1 g 2 f 3 c 4 a 5 h 6 d 7 b 8 e

4
1 g 2 a 3 e 4 f 5 b 6 h 7 d 8 c

5
1 swear 2 fine 3 respect 4 access
5 bill 6 privacy 7 return 8 charge

3D

1
1 what 2 kind 3 call 4 mean 5 heard
6 stand 7 exactly 8 for

2
1 g 2 h 3 a 4 e 5 c 6 d 7 b 8 f

Listening

1
a

2
1 T … I've never been to South Africa.
2 F … I worked in a nature reserve.
3 F … No, I haven't.
4 T … Oh, and you could visit one of the oldest
  buildings in South Africa – The Castle of
  Good Hope.
5 F … I've got no idea!
6 T … She'll get bored if we're on the beach all day.
7 F … No, we haven't, but we'd love to.
8 T … I love it. It's full of interesting spices and
  flavours.

3
1 four 2 three 3 40 4 17th 5 two
6 three 7 three 8 hundreds

Reading

1
It's an article about the discoveries of young
scientists.

2
1 F Jack started doing his research in a school
  laboratory.
2 T
3 F He worked after school, at weekends and
  during the holidays.
4 F Finally, he developed a new test for cancer
5 F … she decided to develop a fuel using plants
  that she grew in her bedroom.
6 F She created her own laboratory … under her
  bed.
7 T
8 T

3
1 He discovered a new test for a particular type
  of cancer cell.
2 15 years old
3 Because it's less expensive and more likely
  to find the cancer cells than any other tests
  which have been used.
4 At the Intel International Science and
  Engineering Fair
5 She discovered a fuel using the plants that
  grow in ponds.
6 17 years old
7 Because it shows how in the future plants
  could be used as fuel instead of oil or gas.
8 the Intel Science Talent Search prize

4
1 B 2 J 3 S 4 J 5 S 6 J 7 B 8 J
9 S 10 J

5
1 d 2 e 3 a 4 g 5 f 6 c 7 b

6
1 b 2 d 3 a 4 c

7
Sara Voltz

8
Advantages: They are renewable so they won't
run out; They don't produce as much pollution as
oil and gas when they are burned.
Disadvantages: They aren't as efficient as oil and
gas, so we have to produce more of them; Making
them uses a lot of water and energy at the moment.

Writing

1
a Summary 1   b Summary 2

2
1 F … studying and living abroad is the only way
  to become a global leader.
2 F … many American degrees don't offer an
  international part of their course.
3 T
4 T
5 F … young women are twice as likely to use
  social media as a way of campaigning on
  issues
  … young men are twice as likely to use it to
  communicate with politicians
6 T

3a
1 ✓ 2 ✗ 3 ✓ 4 ✓ 5 ✓ 6 ✓ 7 ✓ 8 ✗

3b
1 e 2 a 3 c 4 b 5 d

5
argues discusses claims goes on to say
talks about lists ends with explains

6
1 explains 2 talks about 3 lists 4 discusses
5 claims 6 ends with 7 goes on to say
8 argues 9 emphasises the fact 10 lists

7 and 8
Students' own answers

UNIT 4

4A

1
1 a 2 a 3 a 4 b 5 b 6 a 7 b 8 a

2
1 Jane **was looking** in her bag when she walked
  into the streetlight.
2 correct
3 Ellie accidentally **picked up** another woman's
  bag because she thought it was her bag.
4 I was talking on the phone when I **smelled** the
  pizza burning in the oven.
5 As I was lighting the barbecue, my hair
  caught fire.
6 correct
7 I **was trying** an expensive perfume in a shop
  when my phone rang and the bottle slipped
  out of my hand.
8 correct

3
1 was 2 was hurrying 3 was looking
4 got 5 slipped 6 fell 7 tried 8 had to

4
1 slipped 2 flooded 3 spilt 4 caught
5 knocked 6 crashed 7 measured
8 turned

5
1 c 2 a 3 a 4 a 5 b 6 a

4B

1
1 c 2 f 3 d 4 g 5 h 6 e 7 b 8 a

2
1 gang, broke into 2 arrested, get away
3 witness, victim 4 theft, claimed
5 attack, victim 6 trial, freed

3
1 reported 2 jail 3 claimed 4 trap
5 freed 6 worth 7 attack 8 victim

4
1 'd been, met 2 realised, had got in
3 remembered, had already closed
4 'd been, realised 5 'd never, read
6 was, 'd left

5
1 The **gang had disappeared by the time** the
  police arrived.
2 The woman got away in a blue car **after** she
  had **robbed** the garage.
3 Laura was terrified because she **had never
  been** the victim of a crime **before**.
4 Ava didn't realise someone **had stolen** her
  phone **until** she got home.
5 She was on the train **when** she remembered
  that she **hadn't locked** the door.
6 The robber had to go to hospital **because** she
  had been bitten by the guard dog.
7 Nobody noticed that Sam **had left** the party
  until the disco started.
8 The detectives had to get things right this time.
  They **had already made** too many mistakes.

6
1 had already heard 2 was 3 had broken
4 had stolen 5 had lit 6 had attacked
7 were 8 had seen 9 asked 10 had

4C

1
1 loan 2 cracked 3 sort out 4 delivered
5 screen 6 overcharged 7 wi-fi
8 guarantee

2
1 refund 2 fault 3 gone 4 gears
5 sort 6 guarantee 7 exchange

3
1 up 2 off 3 back 4 out 5 with 6 for

4
1 a 2 b 3 b 4 a 5 a 6 b 7 a 8 b

5
1 Greg said that he had got a great deal on his
  phone.
2 I asked if the engine had gone.
3 Gina told me that I should take my tablet back
  and get a refund.
4 She asked if she could have a discount.
5 The sales assistant explained that my
  guarantee had ended.
6 Bob said that they would be getting a
  delivery of new parts soon.
7 The man at the store said that it isn't/wasn't
  my fault that it had broken.
8 I explained that it was making a funny noise.

4D

1
1 That's wonderful news.
2 When will you hear?
3 I hope it all goes OK.
4 I bet you're really excited.
5 Well, you sound like you've made up your mind.
6 I bet you're really angry.
7 When did you hear about it?
8 I hope you get the job.

2
1 e 2 g 3 a 4 b 5 d 6 h 7 c 8 f

Listening

1
a (Jude was a victim of crime. Kim's friend was a
  victim of crime, but Kim wasn't.)

2
1 T I was walking down the high street with my
  friend.
2 F … a motorbike with two people on it came
  out of nowhere
3 F it had her laptop in it.
4 T Did she get her laptop back?/ No.
5 T I suppose it was partly my fault.
6 T I was in Paris, near the Eiffel Tower.
7 F I bet it ruined your holiday./ It did a bit.

8 F *Was your passport in your backpack?/Luckily, it wasn't.*

3
1 Her bag with her laptop in it.
2 She was upset and angry.
3 They had to report the crime to the police.
4 He was a bit embarrassed about it.
5 On the chair next to him.
6 She spilt a bit of her drink on his leg.
7 Quite a lot of money and some souvenirs.
8 Because he just wanted to forget about the crime.

Reading

1
c
2
1 Greta **2** Laila **3** Johnny **4** Cosmo
5 Johnny/Greta **6** Laila **7** Cosmo
3
1 F *I had to wait another eight hours in the airport for the next flight and I had to pay for a new ticket.*
2 T *I had a morning flight back the next day …*
3 T *Now I feel lonely and stressed and I've lost all my confidence.*
4 F *I can't tell my parents because they are so proud that I'm studying.*
5 F *The rabbit has caused a lot of damage to her flat.*
6 F *I just don't know what to do!*
7 F *When it happened, I had been working for my dad's best friend's company for about a year.*
8 T *Because I hadn't realised what I'd done, I pressed 'empty trash' too!*
4
1 ill **2** reading **3** confusing **4** pleased with
5 weather was bad **6** damaged things
7 removed **8** didn't
5
1 inconvenient **2** misread **3** stressed
4 jealous **5** proud **6** files **7** delete
8 destroying
6
1 Greta
7
1 as 'a nightmare'
2 clothes and shoes
3 a fish
4 a carpet (or a rug), an umbrella
5 The person needs a carpet or a rug because the rabbit made holes in the old carpet;
The person needs an umbrella so that he/she doesn't have to shelter in a shop next time it rains.

Writing

1
1 when **2** but **3** However **4** As **5** Then
6 As soon as **7** By the time **8** Despite
2
1 writer's **2** Only one person experiences
3 couldn't **4** shark **5** dropped
6 didn't attack **7** didn't attack **8** took
3
1 b **2** c **3** a **4** c **5** b **6** a **7** b **8** c
5
1 in the sea
2 the writer and a whale
3 sharp, strange, enormous, beautiful, friendly, amazing
4 softly
5 like a sharp knife through butter
6 Panic made me want to swim but my head told me not to move; I began laughing and crying at the same time.
6
1 c **2** e **3** h **4** b **5** g **6** a **7** d **8** f
7–9
Students' own answers

UNIT 5

5A

1
1 a **2** b **3** b **4** c **5** b **6** c **7** a **8** b
2
1 took over **2** profit **3** competitor **4** field
5 wages **6** expand **7** launch **8** export
3
1 a **2** a **3** b **4** b **5** a **6** b **7** a **8** a
4
1 b **2** a **3** b **4** a **5** c **6** c **7** a **8** b
9 b

5B

1
1 I haven't finished my research yet.
2 She's just started a new job.
3 My sister has had five different jobs so far.
4 Sue has even thrown away her TV.
5 We've already visited three different capital cities.
6 We've only been to two countries in Europe.
7 We still haven't decided where to go next year.
8 The students have already left the party.
2
1 a **2** b **3** b **4** a **5** b **6** c **7** b
3
1 struggling **2** quit **3** change my mind
4 offered **5** went ahead **6** got rid of
7 sorted out **8** graduating
4
1 date **2** ceremony **3** permission
4 destination **5** agreed **6** nothing
5
1 sort out **2** graduate **3** struggle **4** date
5 ceremony **6** possession **7** destination

5C

1
positive: succeed, give individual attention, raise standards, encourage someone, maintain discipline
negative: be put off something, put pressure on someone, perform badly
2
1 c **2** b **3** a **4** c **5** a **6** b **7** b **8** c
3
1 h **2** f **3** c **4** e **5** d **6** g **7** b **8** a
4
1 correct
2 correct
3 **Apparently**, 80% of people in my year failed at least one exam.
4 James wanted to go to Sussex University, but **unfortunately**, he wasn't accepted.
5 correct
6 correct
7 **Generally**, girls do better than boys in UK schools.
8 correct

5D

1
1 I don't see it like that.
2 I'm not so sure that's true **3** I guess
4 I suppose so **5** I kind of agree **6** Fair point
2
1 b **2** c **3** a **4** a **5** c **6** a

Listening

1
c

2
1 F *I'm in the process of opening a new restaurant.*
2 F *I was chatting with a chef friend … and we realised we'd created a great idea for a new restaurant of our own.*
3 F *… right in the centre of the old town.*
4 F *It's going to be called 'Green Shoots'.*
5 T *Foraging is when you find and collect food that is growing naturally …*
6 F *… I'll buy the rest of the food from local farms.*
7 F *… the builders realised … that the ceiling wasn't safe.*
8 F *… we're having a launch party on 23rd August.*
3
1 a **2** a **3** b **4** b **5** a **6** a

Reading

1
b
2
a 5 **b** 2 **c** 3 **d** 1 **e** 4
3
1 A **2** F **3** C **4** – **5** B **6** D **7** – **8** E
4
1 society
2 Because the organisation of families has changed and technology has advanced.
3 Eating dinner with their family.
4 Too much time spent on devices.
5 Doing jobs/chores at home.
6 girls **7** travelling **8** abroad
5
1 process **2** influence **3** access
4 well-being **5** limit **6** lack **7** chores
8 open-minded
6
chores around the home
7
1 businesswoman **2** good
3 didn't perform well
4 didn't put pressure on **5** positive
6 chores to do **7** thinks **8** is also

Writing

1
b
2
1 However **2** While **3** As well as
4 For example **5** In short **6** I believe
3
c
4
1 B **2** A **3** D **4** C
5
1 B **2** C **3** D
6
The writer of this essay thinks that the benefits of homeworking outweigh the disadvantages.
7
1 d **2** f **3** a **4** e **5** c
8
1 b **2** a
9
1 While **2** However **3** However **4** While
5 While
10 and 11
Students' own answers

UNIT 6

6A

1
1 of **2** me **3** in **4** off **5** off **6** over
2
1 scene **2** series **3** special effects
4 ending **5** dialogue **6** episode **7** filming
8 blockbuster

3
1 tense 2 hilarious 3 dull 4 useless
5 is a fan of 6 characters

4
1 The series is shown every Wednesday at 8 p.m.
2 The special effects were done in the studio.
3 Famous TV programmes get made in this studio.
4 Actors are being paid more than they used to be.
5 Only one episode had been made before the series was cancelled.
6 This scene is going to be cut from the episode.
7 The new series will be filmed in Europe.
8 This episode has been produced in two weeks.

5
1 Many new TV programmes are made every year.
2 The actor had been offered lots of parts before this one.
3 This TV programme was produced very well.
4 Some actors get/are paid millions of dollars for every film.
5 That character is going to be killed off in the next episode.
6 This episode has been cut up into short scenes.
7 That scene is being filmed at the moment.
8 The new streaming service will be used by millions of people next year.

 6B

1
1 replace 2 deliver 3 assessed 4 fixed
5 did 6 removed 7 look at 8 made

2
1 convenient 2 out of 3 on 4 mess
5 efficient 6 useless 7 trust 8 reliable
9 reasonable

3
1 h 2 a 3 b 4 e 5 c 6 g 7 d 8 f

4
1 has/gets her nails done
2 'm/am having/getting my car fixed
3 had/got a tooth removed
4 had/got his nose broken
5 had/got her passport taken away
6 have/get his tyre replaced
7 've/have had/got my hair done/ 've been having/getting my hair done

5
1 I had my toenails **done** last week.
2 correct
3 correct
4 We had some Chinese food **delivered** an hour ago.
5 correct
6 He **got/had** his wallet stolen yesterday.
7 We're having our house **painted** at the moment.
8 Diane gets **her car cleaned** every month.

 6C

1
1 c 2 g 3 h 4 a 5 f 6 b 7 e 8 d

2
1 union 2 quit 3 breakthrough
4 opinion poll 5 scandal 6 profits
7 sentence 8 strike

3
1 there's a good chance it will
2 It's bound to 3 might 4 definitely won't
5 it's fairly likely that it will
6 He definitely won't 7 He might
8 It'll definitely

4
1 a 2 a 3 b 4 b 5 b 6 a 7 a 8 b

 6D

1
1 really 2 afraid 3 would 4 impossible
5 make 6 least 7 understanding 8 worry

2
1 I'm terribly sorry, but I can't come to the project meeting tomorrow.
2 Honestly, I really can't get out of it.
3 There is really nothing I can do about it at this point.
4 These things happen.
5 Let me assure you that it won't happen again.
6 It is what it is.
7 I can only apologise.
8 I'll make it a priority.

Listening

1
c

2
1 This Beautiful World 2 Martin Harris
3 *True or Terrible* 4 Australia
5 *The Sound Garden* 6 Los Angeles
7 Derek Sams 8 *The Day of Arrival*

3
1 F *… I was nearly in tears …*
2 T *It was so sad and so well acted.*
3 F *Last night, this singer got voted off.*
4 T *I like TV programmes that are well written and characters that you can believe in.*
5 T *It was a drama about two brothers … They run a restaurant together.*
6 F *I wouldn't waste your money on it.*
7 T *It's just so expensive.*
8 T *Well, I'd rather watch films in bed on my laptop.*

Reading

1
Articles A and E feature positive news.

2
1 C 2 D 3 B 4 E 5 A

3
1 C 2 B 3 E 4 D 5 A

4
1 Scientists now understand the genes of some cancers.
2 Doctors will be able to identify which patients are most likely to benefit from new drugs.
3 Several former employees have said this.
4 The company might have hidden the money in bank accounts abroad.
5 They've been advised to check transport websites for more information before they travel.
6 It will probably last until Sunday evening.
7 He was driving too fast.
8 Because if he hadn't slowed down, she would have been killed.
9 Profits have risen by 8 percent.
10 They closed several local banks and hundreds of employees lost their jobs.

5
1 Dr Simon Burrows 2 Northover & Co
3 Morgan Peters 4 Tom Peterson
5 Chesterham United 6 Teresa Raymond
7 New Market Ltd 8 River Rowe

6
1 identify 2 benefit 3 overseas 4 accounts
5 flood 6 pedestrian 7 profits 8 increase

Writing

1
b

2
1 The survey is about sharing images online.
2 It took place last February.
3 A hundred people between the ages of 18 and 65.
4 There are differences between young and old people when it comes to why they share photographs.

5 Any statistic in the report e.g.:
Only fourteen percent of people over the age of 35 share photos of themselves once a week or more.
6 Any example with contrasting words: while, whereas or compared to, e.g.:
Older people are more likely to share photos of holidays, while it is popular for young people to share selfies.
In this example, the things that young and older people share are being contrasted.
7 *People of all ages enjoy sharing images online. Young people like share images to show others how happy they are.*
8 *The survey results suggest that …*

3
1 were interviewed 2 asked 3 while
4 third 5 appears 6 majority 7 compared
8 suggest

4
1 c 2 b 3 d 4 a 5 h 6 e 7 f 8 g

5 and 6
Students' own answers

UNIT 7

7A

1
1 f 2 a 3 b 4 e 5 d 6 c

2
1 d 2 g 3 a 4 f 5 h 6 b 7 e 8 c

3
1 broke 2 throat 3 bruised
4 allergic reaction 5 stiff 6 injured

4
1 My dad has pains in his chest but he's refusing **to see** a doctor.
2 I keep **getting** a pain in my knee.
3 correct
4 correct
5 I don't enjoy **going** to the doctor's.
6 correct
7 I hope **to be out** of hospital by next week.
8 I tried **to find** some information about the disease on the internet.

5
1 1b, 2a 2 1a, 2b 3 1a, 2b 4 1b, 2a

7B

1
1 I bet they'll buy a new car.
2 Do you think Elisa married him for his money?
3 I wonder if Matt earns more than me.
4 Poppy said she would buy dinner tonight.
5 I imagine that he's finding it difficult to pay his rent.
6 Did you say you'd nearly saved enough money?
7 We realised we couldn't afford the new flat.
8 I don't think I should buy another pair of shoes.
9 Do you know where we're meeting Lisa?
10 Chris doesn't know when he'll get a pay increase.

2
1 that 2 if 3 when 4 Do 5 that 6 Do
7 where 8 if

3
1 b 2 c 3 b 4 a 5 a 6 c 7 a 8 c

4
1 to buy 2 earning 3 afford 4 to lend
5 take 6 paid 7 owe 8 to win

5
1 earnings 2 debt 3 payment 4 wealth
5 rate 6 afford

1

the height of the buildings, firefighters, traffic jams, emergency fire services, fire engines, the site of a fire, fire services, jet skis, jet packs, fire hose

2

1 It doesn't seem right that buses in the UK don't have **seat belts**.
2 correct
3 correct
4 correct
5 The queue at **passport control** was enormous.
6 To hire a car you need to have a **driving licence**.
7 I parked the car and Mum went to get the **car park ticket**.
8 The **traffic noise** is deafening on Station Road.

3

1 car crash 2 bus stop 3 petrol station
4 shopping bags 5 public transport
6 traffic laws 7 breakdown service
8 lorry drivers

4

1 driving test 2 footpath 3 petrol station
4 flat tyre 5 lorry driver
6 breakdown service 7 motorbike helmet

5

1 control 2 gear 3 crashed 4 helmet
5 fine 6 park 7 points 8 pulled out
9 engine 10 brake

1

1 way 2 supposed 3 nothing 4 me
5 appreciate 6 strictly 7 could 8 helpful

2

1 Let me see what I can do.
2 I really appreciate it.
3 Is there really nothing you can do?
4 You'd be doing me a huge favour.
5 Let me speak to my manager.
6 I can't thank you enough.

Listening

1

c

2

1 F I got back on Saturday.
2 F It's just south of the Yangtze River.
3 T Have you been to Venice then?
      Yes, I have actually.
4 F And of course the famous vaporetti,
      which is the water taxi ...
      Gondolas are just for tourists.
5 F I've been to Mexcaltitán in Mexico.
6 T It's built on a man-made island.
7 F I'd really like to go to Ganvie in Benin.
8 F The people who live there travel around in
      canoes called pirogues.

3

1 7,000 2 118 3 1,600 4 400 5 800
6 3,000

Reading

1

1 Ben 2 Catherine 3 Jemima 4 Yuri
5 Louise

2

1 Because they need help immediately and
   don't have time to make an appointment.
2 Catherine
3 Catherine and Yuri
4 Catherine and Ben
5 Because his patients (the animals) can't tell
   him what's wrong.
6 Yuri
7 She thinks she's not good at talking to people.
8 Jemima
9 Louise
10 Yuri

3

1 appointment 2 patients 3 hygiene
4 can't stand 5 a matter of life or death
6 operation 7 social club 8 sociable

4

b

5

1 c 2 a 3 d 4 b

Writing

1

Email 1 is formal. Email 2 is informal.

2

1 on 2 at 3 off 4 at 5 ahead 6 after
7 up 8 by 9 by 10 in 11 on 12 on

3

Email 1

1 T The taxis are right outside the station but
      the buses are 100 metres away.
2 F
3 T Go all the way to the seafront ...
4 T Clarence Villa is on the fourth street on
      your left, just after the Majestic Hotel.
5 F The meter is about halfway up the street.
6 T

Email 2

7 F Don't think I've sent you directions to my
      new flat.
8 T ... get the District Line to East Putney ...
      and keep walking for about 200 metres.
9 F you'll pass a French restaurant on your left
      – don't stop to eat there! It's very expensive.
10 T It's a side street, so make sure you don't
      miss it!
11 F I'm right at the top of the building!
12 T See you on Sunday.

4

Email 1

1–4 any of the following: seafront, the clock
      tower, The George pub, the racecourse,
      the park, St Cuthbert's Church, Brighton Pier,
      the Majestic Hotel
5 Walk straight ahead for about 100 metres.
6 ... follow the edge of the park for about
   300 metres.
7 ... you'll be able to see the sea ahead of you.
8 You should be able to see Brighton Pier to the
   right.

Email 2

1 French restaurant
2 post box
3 ... keep walking for about 200 metres.
4 ... keep walking in the same direction for
   another 500 metres.
5 If you're standing with your back to the
   station ...
6 If you're facing the house ...

5

1 entrance 2 facing 3 off 4 direction
5 subway 6 roundabout 7 halfway
8 fork 9 approach 10 side

1

1 c 2 a 3 h 4 g 5 b 6 d 7 f 8 e

2

1 natural disasters 2 floods
3 climate change 4 consuming 5 recycle
6 waste 7 pollution 8 reproducing
9 prevent 10 die out

3

1 f 2 h 3 d 4 b 5 g 6 e 7 a 8 c

4

1 even if 2 if 3 in case 4 unless
5 even if 6 in case 7 unless 8 if

5

1 won't cause 2 will still be 3 might reduce
4 'll save energy 5 might die out
6 shouldn't go 7 will make 8 takes

1

1 Please talk to me whenever you need to.
2 Take this with you wherever you go.
3 Whatever the time, Yasmin is always ready to
   talk.
4 Richard is nasty to me whenever I see him.
5 However hard Kamil works, he never does well
   in exams.
6 Wherever Marissa goes, people love her!
7 My dad is always reliable, whatever the
   situation.
8 Whoever you speak to, you should be polite.

2

1 a 2 c 3 a 4 b 5 b 6 a 7 b 8 b

3

1 however 2 whenever 3 whatever
4 Wherever 5 whoever 6 however
7 Whenever

4

1 politically 2 reliable 3 racist
4 confidence 5 calm 6 willing 7 nasty
8 bright

5

1 sweet 2 talented 3 difficult 4 active
5 generous 6 strict 7 patient 8 reliable

1

1 e 2 h 3 d 4 g 5 a 6 b 7 c 8 f

2

1 retired 2 mortgage 3 partner
4 graduated 5 pregnant 6 birth 7 married
8 together

3

1 a, death 2 g, retirement 3 c, engagement
4 h, separation 5 b, divorce 6 f, pregnancy
7 e, marriage 8 d, graduation

4

1 Once 2 As soon as 3 until 4 When
5 After 6 until 7 after 8 before

5

1 arrived 2 graduation 3 retired
4 isn't going to look 5 announced
6 marriage 7 is going to move/is moving
8 have/'ve paid off

1

1 calling 2 through 3 How 4 ringing
5 do 6 problem 7 if 8 hold

2

1 reached 2 for 3 ringing 4 wondered
5 to 6 extension 7 interested 8 know

Listening

1

b

2

1 c 2 b 3 b 4 b 5 a 6 a 7 b 8 a

3

1 Because her mother is English, her father is
   Spanish and she grew up in Italy, so they spoke
   all three languages at home.
2 Because she grew up surrounded by books in
   her house.
3 To see if she could write a good book and get it
   published.
4 Because they were frightened to publish a
   book by a new author.
5 Because she is grateful that they took a
   chance on her with her first book.
6 Because she was busy with her two young
   children.
7 Because her experiences helped her to grow
   up during her thirties. Her father died, she and
   her husband got divorced and she was alone
   with two children.

8 Because work was going well, she was happy in a new relationship and her children were enjoying school. (She realised it was going to be OK.)

Reading

1
b

2
Students' own answers

3
1 F *The questionnaire is about how you behave.*
2 T *A friend of yours made some racist comments as part of a joke.*
3 F *Your boss has become politically active, but all her conversations are about politics now and it's starting to annoy the employees.*
4 T *An elderly relative, who lives alone, phones you just as you're going out to meet a friend.*
5 F *A friend suddenly stops answering your text messages and emails*
6 T *You have a difficult relationship with your mother-in-law …*
7 T
8 F *We may not be scientists …*

4
1 Mostly Cs   **2** Mostly As   **3** Mostly Bs
Results: Students' own answers

5
1 Mostly Bs   **2** Mostly As   **3** Mostly Cs

6
1 mostly   **2** opinion   **3** hardly ever
4 relative   **5** upset   **6** avoid   **7** honest
8 argument

Writing

1
A and B

2
1 D   **2** B   **3** C   **4** A

3
1 Dinner will be served
2 Thank you very much for the invitation
3 If there's anything you don't eat
4 Nothing could keep me away!
5 No meat for me, please.

4
1 You are warmly invited
2 the summer party is held
3 Drinks will be served
4 dinner will start
5 Dress code: formal
6 Should you require
7 include this in your RSVP
8 RSVP

5
1 c   **2** b   **3** b   **4** c   **5** a   **6** b   **7** a   **8** c

6
1 e   **2** f   **3** a   **4** c   **5** d   **6** b

7 and **8**
Students' own answers

 UNIT 9

 9A

1
1 g   **2** h   **3** f   **4** d   **5** e   **6** b   **7** a   **8** c

2
1 communities   **2** spaces   **3** violence
4 pressure   **5** generous   **6** fact of life
7 wages   **8** part-time   **9** discrimination
10 tolerance

3
1 I wish I could afford to work part-time.
2 I wish there were more police on our streets.
3 We wish we could afford to move.
4 I wish they would collect the rubbish more often.
5 I wish Noor didn't have to work weekends.

6 I wish people weren't so rude.
7 I wish I didn't have to go to work today.
8 I wish this traffic jam would move.

4
1 worked   **2** would   **3** would   **4** could
5 lived   **2** could   **7** had   **8** would

5
1 I wish I could go to the party (tonight).
2 I wish the council would mend the benches in the park.
3 I wish I knew what to do.
4 I wish the train company would put more trains on.
5 I wish I had my own car.
6 I wish there were streetlights by the beach.
7 I wish I could help Ollie.
8 I wish it was hot and sunny.

 9B

1
1 b   **2** a   **3** j   **4** g   **5** d   **6** e   **7** h   **8** f
9 c   **10** i

2
1 taken   **2** ruled   **3** majority   **4** peace
5 put   **6** rid   **7** homeless   **8** healthcare
9 fund

3
1 c   **2** f   **3** a   **4** h   **5** b   **6** g   **7** d   **8** e

4
1 If people didn't **have** to work, they would get very bored.
2 If you **were** a millionaire, what would you spend your money on?
3 What **would** you do if you lost your job?
4 If I **had written** *The Hunger Games*, I would be a very rich woman now.
5 If I had a better imagination, I **might/may/ would** be able to imagine a world like that.
6 If I lived in a world ruled by robots, I **would** fight to take control.
7 I might think I was dreaming if I **woke** up to find that everyone in society was equal.
8 What rules **would** you make if you were asked to create a perfect society?

9C

1
1 must   **2** might   **3** can't   **4** must   **5** can't
6 must   **7** can't   **8** can't

2
1 must   **2** can't   **3** must   **4** must   **5** must
6 might

3
positive: break the record time, in the lead
negative: come last, get beaten, get knocked out, get sent off, miss a penalty

4
1 b   **2** g   **3** c   **4** d   **5** e   **6** a   **7** h   **8** f

5
1 drowned   **2** train   **3** sent
4 got beaten   **5** break   **6** come last

9D

1
1 could   **2** mind   **3** about   **4** go   **5** worries
6 back   **7** interrupt   **8** point

2
1 Could I just say something there?
2 Sorry, but I just wanted to make a quick suggestion.
3 Thanks for pointing that out.
4 Anyway, sorry to interrupt.
5 So, as I was saying
6 Do you mind if I come in here?
7 So you were saying?
8 Could I just stop you there for a moment?

Listening

1
b

2
1, 3, 4 and 6

3
1 b   **2** b   **3** b   **4** b   **5** a   **6** a   **7** b   **8** a

Reading

1
c

2
1 E   **2** B   **3** C   **4** D   **5** A

3
1 F   *They were Spanish.*
2 T
3 F   *He was Spanish.*
4 F   *His family was wealthy.*
5 T
6 F   *… he agreed with Thomas More's ideas.*
7 F   *He was sent to prison in Spain for the rest of his life.*
8 F   *Quiroga used his own money … .*

4
1 Mexico   **2** communities   **3** lawyer
4 in his sixties   **5** disagreed with
6 hospital-school   **7** Bishop of Michoacan
8 schools, hospitals

5
1 appreciated   **2** forced   **3** opportunity
4 dream   **5** mistreating   **6** escape   **7** chaos
8 region

6
c

7
b

8
1 Avatar
2 2009
3 On an alien moon called Pandora.
4 Three-metre-high blue alien people who live on Pandora.
5 They don't try to control them. They ask their permission to fly or ride them.
6 selfish
7 the love story between Neytiri and Jake
8 He's a soldier.

Writing

1
b

2
1 because   **2** that   **3** As a result   **4** So
5 because   **6** so   **7** Since   **8** As a result

3
1 Granny May
2 Because she caught a virus and got very sick.
3 Because she couldn't see her friend as often as she used to.
4 She saw an advert.
5 Two days a week.
6 Because it had snowed.
7 two months
8 They FaceTimed each other.

4
1 It was terrible
2 we all wore coats
3 so Dad had to carry her to the car
4 the party ended at 10 p.m.
5 she wasn't at the wedding
6 Granny May looked amazing
7 Ralph couldn't hear anything
8 they are going to live in Ralph's house

5
1 c   **2** d   **3** a   **4** b   **5** f   **6** e

6
1 The tickets were so expensive that we decided not to go.
2 The schools were closed due to the dangerous weather conditions.
3 They changed the wedding venue as it was so small.

4 Because of the high demand, the show sold out.

5 They were so tired that they decided not to join the other group.

6 She had to stay in Napoli an extra night as the flight was cancelled.

7 Since they had never met before, they were a little shy with each other.

8 Due to the hot weather, they decided not to go outside.

7 and **8**
Students' own answers

UNIT 10

10A

1
1 c **2** h **3** i **4** a **5** b **6** f **7** g **8** d
9 e **10** j

2
1 victories **2** gold medals **3** designed
4 works **5** defended **6** sailing **7** right
8 widely read

3
1 hadn't been, wouldn't have believed
2 had never existed, might never have been
3 had worked, would have
4 had been, would have
5 might not have read, hadn't gone
6 might have studied, had had
7 hadn't missed, have met

4
1 had followed
2 would never have designed
3 hadn't had
4 would never have got
5 hadn't been
6 wouldn't have spent
7 would never have worked
8 hadn't left
9 may never have won
10 hadn't designed

10B

1
1 d **2** g **3** f **4** a **5** c **6** b **7** h **8** e

2
1 deadline **2** rush **3** standard
4 volunteered **5** task **6** manage
7 situation **8** opposition **9** introduce
10 results **11** action **12** forced

3
1 We should **have** finished this last week.
2 We probably should have **extended** the deadline.
3 We shouldn't **have made** William team leader.
4 correct
5 correct
6 correct
7 She shouldn't have **got** such a bad grade.
8 They shouldn't **have** forced us to change it at this stage.

4
1 should have told
2 shouldn't have lied
3 should have guessed
4 should have done
5 should have asked
6 should have talked
7 shouldn't have ignored
8 should have realised

10C

1
1 value **2** set **3** last **4** stylish **5** feature
6 automatically **7** complicated **8** ideal

2
1 leather **2** lasted **3** bargain **4** room
5 decent **6** designed **7** automatically
8 tough

3
1 It's a **big red American** car.
2 I love your **enormous blue and orange Moroccan** carpet.
3 Have you seen Laila's **big new gold** ring?
4 Harriet's got a pairs of **fantastic grey leather** boots
5 It's a **beautiful tiny wooden** table.
6 Mr French always wears a **disgusting old red** jumper
7 My neighbour has got a **cute little black and white** puppy.
8 I've just bought a **lovely big Italian** sofa for my apartment.

4
1 mild white Italian
2 lovely red leather
3 dirty small yellow
4 stylish modern silver
5 wonderful new Spanish
6 strange little grey
7 big old brown
8 original Mexican clay
9 lovely long woollen
10 comfortable old blue

5
1 ancient **2** stone **3** ridiculous **4** little
5 French **6** black and white

10D

1
1 Would **2** Please **3** help **4** manage
5 Shall **6** kind **7** hand **8** mind **9** free
10 great

2
1 happy **2** worry **3** welcome **4** fine
5 sure **6** need **7** offer **8** Let

Listening

1
b

2
1 c **2** c **3** a **4** c **5** a **6** b **7** a **8** c

3
1 red **2** (really) comfortable **3** bed
4 put it together **5** eight **6** confusing
7 orange **8** two years

Reading

1
b

2
b

3
1 artist **2** philosopher **3** explorers
4 military engineer **5** military leader

4
1 15 paintings
2 he wrote them backwards (from right to left)
3 the technology had not yet been developed
4 in 1499
5 Cesare Borgia
6 They think he deliberately designed them not to work because he didn't want to hurt others.
7 So that he could be remembered for a long time.

5
1 contribution **2** talent **3** outline
4 equipment **5** flow **6** sink **7** inventions
8 extraordinary

6
He was learning about worms and how they move.

7
1 T
2 F *... Then he heard about a natural disaster ... in a nearby city.*
3 T *David wondered if it might be possible to design a robot worm that could go underground and rescue people.*
4 T
5 F *David designed his robot and won an award for it.*

6 T *He knew that mosquitoes lay their eggs in water and the chemicals we use to kill them can pollute the water we drink.*
7 F *David designed a robot to collect and then kill young mosquitoes from the surface of the water ...*
8 T *He thought about how other mosquitoes can carry dangerous diseases.*
9 T *After this success, David started work on designing a different robot to solve another problem.*

Writing

1
positive

2
1 c **2** a **3** b

3
1 F *He wrote at least 37 plays and a collection of poems*
2 T *William Shakespeare is considered one of the greatest English language writers and poets*
3 F *He was born in 1564 in Stratford-up on-Avon ...*
4 F *... and they had three children together ...*
5 F *In 1594, he joined a theatre group called The Lord Chamberlain's Men.*
6 T *... Shakespeare's plays were also per formed at the royal court in front of Queen Elizabeth I and King James I.*
7 F *Shakespeare used 15,000 words in his plays ...*
8 T *They claim that Shakespeare's use of language was so rich that if he hadn't written his plays, the English language would not contain many of the words we use to say how we are feeling or to talk about our experiences.*
9 T *It can be seen in the titles of popular songs, books, plays and films, such as Agatha Christie's 'The Mousetrap' and Alfred Hitchcock's 'North by Northwest', both of which have titles taken from Shakespeare plays.*
10 T *His influence can also be seen in thousands of English sayings, such as to have 'a heart of gold'.*

4
1 As well as **2** Furthermore
3 Not only, but also

5
1 b **2** a **3** c

6
1 Shakespeare not only performed in front of Elizabeth I, but also James I.
2 As well as tragedies, Shakespeare wrote comedies and histories.
3 Shakespeare wrote a lot of amazing plays. Furthermore, he wrote many beautiful poems.

8
1 e **2** b **3** a **4** f **5** c **6** d

9 and **10**
Students' own answers